EDMUND BURKE
1729–1797
A Bibliography

Recent Titles in
Bibliographies of British Statesmen

William Pitt the Younger 1759–1806: A Bibliography
A. D. Harvey

Lord Grenville 1759–1834: A Bibliography
A. D. Harvey

Lord Curzon 1839–1925: A Bibliography
James G. Parker

Lord Nelson 1758–1805: A Bibliography
Leonard W. Cowie

The Duke of Wellington 1769–1852: A Bibliography
Michael Partridge

Charles James Fox 1749–1806: A Bibliography
David Schweitzer

George Grenville 1712–1770: A Bibliography
Rory T. Cornish

William Wilberforce 1759–1833: A Bibliography
Leonard W. Cowie

Margaret Thatcher: A Bibliography
Faysal Mikdadi

William Pitt, Earl of Chatham, 1708–1778: A Bibliography
Karl W. Schweizer

Lord Palmerston, 1784–1865: A Bibliography
Michael S. Partridge and Karen E. Partridge

EDMUND BURKE
1729–1797
A Bibliography

Leonard W. Cowie

BIBLIOGRAPHIES OF
BRITISH STATESMEN, NO. 19

GREGORY PALMER, SERIES EDITOR

Greenwood Press
Westport, Connecticut • London

Library of Congress Cataloging-in-Publication Data

Cowie, Leonard W.
     Edmund Burke, 1729–1797 : a bibliography / Leonard W. Cowie.
        p. cm.—(Bibliographies of British statesmen, ISSN
  1056–5523 ; no. 19)
     Includes indexes.
     ISBN 0–313–28710–4 (alk. paper)
     1. Burke, Edmund, 1729–1797—Bibliography. 2. Great Britain—
Politics and government—1760–1820—Bibliography. I. Title.
II. Series.
Z8133.23.C67   1994
[DA506.B9]
016.94107′3′092—dc20   93–45955

British Library Cataloguing in Publication Data is available.

Library of Congress Catalog Card Number: 93–45955
ISBN: 0–313–28710–4
ISSN: 1056–5523

First published in 1994

Greenwood Press, 88 Post Road West, Westport, CT 06881
An imprint of Greenwood Publishing Group, Inc.

Printed in the United States of America

The paper used in this book complies with the
Permanent Paper Standard issued by the National
Information Standards Organization (Z39.48–1984).

10 9 8 7 6 5 4 3 2

Contents

Introduction

Edmund Burke (1729-1797) was born in Dublin, Ireland, and came to London in 1750 to study law, which he abandoned in order to take up writing. He devoted himself to the solution of the political and economic problems of the time and showed himself to be a defender of. the established order of society. During this time, he was a member of the distinguished group of writers and artists which gathered around Dr. Johnson. He began his career as an active politician in 1756 when he became private secretary to the Marquis of Rockingham and a Member of Parliament. He urged a policy of conciliation with the American colonies and took a leading part in the impeachment of Warren Hastings for corruption in India. He supported the movement for political and economic reform in the government of the kingdom. On the outbreak of the French Revolution, he attacked its destructive purposes and breach of historical continuity.

Burke was both an active politician and a political thinker. Though he only held minor office in two ministries, he strongly affected contemporary opinion. Moreover, his ideas profoundly moulded the future. Particularly he established the basis of the party system and the conservative tradition in democratic politics.

This bibliography is concerned with both these aspects of Burke's life and career. The first two following sections present a guide to this. The Biographical Essay contains an outline of his life showing how his writings and actions were related to his outlook upon the main issues of his time and the reaction he adopted towards them. The Chronology sets out the important events in his life together with the relevant contemporary national and international occurrences which had an effect upon him.

The section on Manuscript and Archival Resources gives the location of the various collections of papers relating to Burke and indicates which are the most important of them. It includes also the relevant <u>Reports</u> and <u>Appendices</u> issued by the <u>Historical Manuscripts Commission</u>. This is followed by a list of such catalogues and guides that have been issued to material about Burke. Finally, the necessary Contemporary Newspapers and Journals are mentioned.

The Section on Published Resources provides a list of the several biographies of Burke and studies of his political thought, together with an account of the resources that have been used by their writers and their consequent present-day value. This is arranged in chronological order of publication as also are the numerous Articles and Essays which have appeared in books and periodicals.

The Section on Writings by Burke begins with the published collections of his works and a list of the articles, speeches and letters with the dates on which he published them. This is followed by the collections of the letters written and received by him and various other books in which some are to be found. The few poems written by Burke in his younger years are also included here.

The Section on the Contemporaries of Burke includes not only those political figures with whom he was closely involved during his active, official life, but also those men and women whom he came to know as a result of the wide and full literary, artistic and social life which he led in London. For each of them there is a brief biographical note and an indication of the most important material about them; and their connection with Burke and his relationship with them is explained.

The Section on the Political Background explains, from the point of view of contemporary British politics, the nature of five important issues in which Burke was involved - the parliamentary parties; administrative and political reform; the American War of Independence; the East india Company; and the French Revolution. Each of these is in the form of an explanatory essay and a short bibliography.

The Section on Burke's Life and Career, which is arranged in chronological order, gives precise indications to important events in both primary and secondary sources. This includes both material which has already been described in preceding sections and material mentioned in it for the first time.

The Section on Burke's Speeches includes those which he made both in Parliament and elsewhere as well as the collections and parliamentary reports in which they may be found, along with a list of those which Burke published during his lifetime.

The Section on the Contemporary Portraits of Burke lists their present whereabouts; and a bibliography enables descriptions of the many Cartoons of him to be found. Places associated with Burke are those in which he lived, studied, visited or worked. His connection with each is described together with its location and present condition.

Abbreviations

BL   British Library.

BN   Bertram Newman, _Edmund Burke_
        (see no. 182)

BOD   Bodleian Library, Oxford.

CEB   _The Correspondence of Edmund Burke_.
        (see no. 424)

CUP   Cambridge University Press.

HMC   Historical Manuscript Commission _Reports_.

HMSO   Her Majesty's Stationary Office.

JP   James Prior, _The Life of the Right Honourable Edmund
        Burke_.
        (see no. 160)

OUP   Oxford University Press.

PB   _The Public and Domestic Life of the Right Honourable
        Edmund Burke_.
        (see no. 162)

PD   _Parliamentary Debates_.
        (see no. 620)

PH   _Parliamentary History_.
        (see no. 621)

PM   Philip Magnus, _Edmund Burke_.
        (see no. 185).

PR   _Parliamentary Register_.
        (see no. 622)

RM   Robert H. Murray, _Edmund Burke_.
        (see no. 183).

4   Edmund Burke

S   The Senator.
         (see no. 623)

SPCK   Society for Promoting Christian Knowledge.

SA   Stanley Ayling, Edmund Burke, His Life and Opinions
         (see no. 227).

WEB   Works of Edmund Burke (Bohn Ed.).
         (see no. 359).

         Unless otherwise mentioned, books are published in London.

Biographical Essay

Edmund Burke was born in Dublin on 12th. January 1729, the second son of Richard Burke, a Protestant attorney, and Mary Nagle, a Roman Catholic and a distant connection of the sixteenth-century poet, Edmund Spenser. They had fifteen children, but only Garrett (c.1725-1765), Edmund (1729-1797), Richard (1733-1794) and Juliana (1738-1790) survived. As was customary in those days, the sons were brought up in the faith of their father and the daughter in that of her mother. Edmund was to be a firm member of the Church of England and a believer in the need for the unity of Church and State.

When he was young, Edmund suffered from weak health, and life in the country was thought to be desirable for him. From approximately the ages of six and eleven he spent most of the time with his grandfather and other maternal relations at Ballyduff in County Cork and was taught at a nearby school held in a ruined castle, once a stronghold of the Nagles (see no. 582).

In 1741, Edmund and his brothers, Garrett and Richard, attended a school kept by Abraham Shackleton, a Yorkshire Quaker, at Ballitore, a village in County Kildare about twenty miles south of Dublin. After three years of classical education, he left Ballitore and entered Trinity College, Dublin (also known as the University of Dublin), and was made a scholar in 1746. While at Trinity, he read widely in history, moral philosophy and literature and proceeded to the degree of B.A. in 1748 and M.A. in 1751. He was later presented with the honorary degree of LL.D. in 1790.

Richard Burke wished his son to become a barrister (a lawyer entitled to appear in the superior courts of England). He was accordingly entered in 1747 as a student at the Middle Temple, one of the legal societies in London which have the exclusive right of admitting persons to practise in these courts In 1750 he went to London to study law. His health still troubled him, however, and Burke did not find his legal studies attractive. This neglect resulted in the discontinuance of the allowance from his father in 1755 and so he took to supporting himself by writing essays and articles for for newspapers and magazines. His first separate publication, A Vindication of Natural Society or A View of the Miseries and Evils Arising to Mankind from Every Species of Artificial Society, appeared in 1756. This was an anonymous octavo pamphlet of 106 pages occasioned by the publication in 1753 of the writings of the statesman, Henry St. John, Viscount Bolingbroke (1678-1751), which were hostile to Christianity. Burke set out ironically to confute Bolingbroke by imitating his approach and style to show that his system of reasoning could be used with equal application and falsity to attack any institution, whether human or divine.

This was followed, a few months later, by another anonymous publication, A Philosophical Inquiry into the Origin of our Ideas of the Sublime and Beautiful, an essay in aesthetics after Addison. His purpose was to discover the relevant standards of excellence that should be applied in judging any form of art. This work was a turning-point in Burke's reputation and life as it rapidly gained him recognition and friendship from Sir Joshua Reynolds, Dr. Samuel Johnson, Oliver Goldsmith and other prominent literary and artistic figures.

These two tentative excursions into literature are not of themselves important, but they provide intimations of his personal convictions. They forecast that fact that feeling rather than reason was to be the power that moved him.

Later in 1753 Burke married Jane Mary Nugent, the daughter of an Irish physician practising in Bath, with whom Burke had consulted when visiting there in search of better health. She was a Roman Catholic, but became an Anglican. Their son Richard was born in 1758 and followed by Christopher, who died in infancy. Despite his continued writing, for a time Burke was dependent upon the support of his father-in-law.

By now his mind was turning from abstract speculation to participation in the political and economic affairs of the time. He wrote An Abridgement of the History of England, which was partially printed during 1757, but not published in full until after his death. Burke's public career began in 1759 when, after unsuccessfully applying for the post of British consul at Madrid, he began to earn a regular income when he was engaged by Robert Dodsley (see nos. 380, 589), a writer and bookseller, to be the first editor of the Annual Register. This volume was published as a record of information on literature, art, science and news of the current year, and Burke contributed to it until 1788. In 1759 he became private secretary to William Gerard Hamilton, a Member of Parliament who was Chief Secretary for Ireland in 1761 to 1764 and Chancellor of the Irish Exchequer from 1763 to 1784. Burke was in Ireland with him from 1761 to 1762 and again from 1763 to 1764. Burke obtained from him in 1763 a pension of £300 a year, but resigned both post and pension in 1764, having quarrelled with him over the terms of his employment. The next year he inherited from his elder brother, Garrett, a small estate in Ireland, which he sold in 1790.

In July 1765 the Marquess of Rockingham, who was by hereditary wealth one of the most powerful men in England, became First Lord of the Treasury and headed a new ministry. He appointed Burke, now a well-known member of society to be his private secretary and from time to time helped him with advances of money and destroyed his bonds at his death in 1782. Through the influence of Ralph, second Earl Verney

(1712?-1791), a wealthy Irish peer and influential Buckinghamshire landowner, Burke entered Parliament in 1765 as a Member for the borough of Wendover in Buckinghamshire. He made his maiden speech early in 1766, speaking on the American question and obtaining immediate recognition as an accomplished orator, even from those in the House of Commons who differed from him. He was responsible for much of the organization which ensured the repeal of the Stamp Act (by which American legal documents and newspapers had to bear stamps). He was always proud of the part he played in it, believing that the repeal could have offered a sensible and lasting solution to the American problem. The Rockingham ministry, however, lasted for only a year, and he was succeeded by the Duke of Grafton with William Pitt (later the Earl of Chatham) in the cabinet. Burke received the offer of a post from the ministry, but he declined it and remained in opposition, vehemently attacking the new administration, particularly over their dealing with the East Indian and American questions in 1766 and 1767. He also wrote and published in 1766 A Short Account of a Late Short Administration, a defence of the Rockingham ministry.

In 1767 Burke received the freedom of the City of Dublin, and in May of the next year a general election resulted in his re-election as Member of Parliament for Wendover. Meanwhile, he had taken part in speculating in East India stock with his brother, Richard, his friend, William Burke (called by him 'cousin' though not a relation), and Lord Verney, but their venture failed in 1769. He was partly involved in their ruin and remained in continuous financial difficulties throughout his life, though he was helped by his appointment in 1771 as London agent for the province of New York. Before the crash came he bought Gregories, a country house near Beaconsfield (see no. 600). He had previously sought rural retreats in Parson's Green in Middlesex and Plaistow in Essex, which were then villages near to London. Beaconsfield remained his rural retreat for the rest of his life, though he continued to live in various houses in London as well (see no. 599).

In 1770 Lord North succeeded Grafton, and Burke continued to be active in opposition. In 1771 he published Thoughts on the Cause of the Present Discontents, perhaps the best-known of his political pamphlets and one of the most influential ever written. It appeared in the midst of the tumult caused by the crisis of John Wilkes and the Middlesex election. Its purpose was to attack the 'influence' of the Crown and uphold the cause of the Rockingham Whigs. Burke himself was bitterly and completely falsely attacked for writing the anonymous Letters of Junius, the fiercest political satire of the century, which appeared in the Public Advertiser between November 1768 and January 1772. They are generally thought to have been written by Sir Philip Francis (1740-1818), then a clerk at the War Office. He later helped Burke prepare charges against Warren Hastings for misgovernment in India.

When the general election of 1774 came, Lord Verney's financial situation prevented him continuing to secure Burke's return for Wendover. He was both nominated to the borough of Malton in Yorkshire by Rockingham and elected by the city of Bristol, whose citizens had been hard-hit by the

the American colonies' ban on British trade. These people were attracted by his efforts to bring the dispute to an end, including the speech on American taxation which he had made that year. Burke accepted his nomination at Bristol to show that he represented some real public opinion, and until the outbreak of war in 1775 he continually strived to obtain conciliation with the colonies. In his attacks on Lord North's conduct of affairs he found a powerful ally in Charles James Fox, and together they exploited the worsening situation in America.

The next few years he devoted himself to plans for economic reform and to pleading for Roman Catholic relief. In 1773 he voted in Parliament for the removal of the legal disabilities of Protestant Dissenters and advocated absentee Irish landlords (mostly living in England). In that year he also visited Paris and returned alarmed by the atheism of the opponents of the French government. He strongly advocated peace with America and in 1778 delivered his great speech condemning the employment of Indians against the colonists in the war. In 1780 he urged economical reform in the public service and restrictions on the African slave trade.

Meanwhile, Burke had became actively involved in the case of Admiral Augustus Keppel (1725-1786). An adherent of the Rockingham Whigs, Keppel was appointed Commander-in-Chief of the Grand Fleet in 1778, which was engaged in blockading Brest. In July he fought an indecisive action against the French fleet off Ushant and was court-martialed for failing in his duty. Burke accompanied him to Portsmouth and assisted in arranging his defence. The charges against him were dismissed as 'malicious and ill-founded,' which was a blow to the ministry.

Burke's support for Irish trade and Roman Catholic emancipation lost him the favour of the citizens of Bristol, who refused to continue supporting him as their member at the general election of 1780. Rockingham again, however, had him elected for Malton, which he accepted and represented for the rest of his political career. He again advocated economical reform and in 1781 was appointed to a Select Committee on Justice in India and became its leading member.

The worsening situation in America encouraged discontent in Ireland, and the Rockingham Whigs exploited both to their advantage. Burke continued his attacks on the conduct of the War and received the freedom of Londonderry. The news of the surrender of Cornwallis at Yorktown in November made North's position impossible, so he resigned in March 1781. He was succeeded by Rockingham. Burke was kept out of the Cabinet by The aristocratic Whigs and George III (who mistrusted him because of his activities in opposition) kept Burke outof the Cabinet, but he was appointed Paymaster of the Forces and was made a Privy Councillor.

During the short time he was in office, he met with some success in urging a policy of conciliation towards Ireland such as he believed would have succeeded in America. Two statutes, Poyning's Act of 1494 and the Declaratory Act of 1719, which placed the Irish Parliament under British control, were repealed in 1782.

But he achieved some success in implementing his ideas of economical reform and reducing the influence of the Crown in

the government of the country. And he took important measures
in connection with his office. The Paymaster-General of of
the Forces was responsible for all money paid to the army and
navy, but was not required to separate such official funds
from his own private cash. Burke was responsible for an act
reforming this situation, which provided that these funds
were to be kept at the Bank of England in an account from
which the Paymaster could make drawings only for official
purposes. By means of another act he transferred regimental
recruitment and finance from the local commanders to the
government, a step which was later to make possible further
improvements in military administration.

Burke's period of office terminated when the ministry was
brought to an end after barely three months by the death of
Rockingham in   July 1782. He   was succeeded by the Earl of
Shelburne, who kept power only until February 1783. Burke
resumed the office of Paymaster-General of the Forces under
the Duke of Portland. By now he had turned his attention to
India. In June 1783 he drew up the comprehensive Ninth Report
of the Select Committee of the House of Commons for enquiring
into the administration of justice in Bengal and other
provinces; and he was largely responsible for drawing up
Fox's India Bill, which brought about the downfall of the
ministry in December 1783.

With the government's dismissal, Burke was again without
office, and this time it was   permanent. William Pitt the
Younger gained power and kept it for the rest of Burke's life
and beyond. Much of Burke's attention became   concentrated
upon the alleged misdeeds of Warren Hastings, who returned to
England in 1785 after being the Governor-General of Bengal.
He was determined to bring Hastings to justice. At first his
chance of success seemed small, but the opposition took up
the question, and ultimately the impeachment moved by Fox was
accepted by Pitt. In 1788 Burke made his famous opening
speech on the impeachment and continued to take part in the
lengthy trial until the acquittal of Hastings in 1795.
Politically the trial harmed the opposition and diverted
their   attention   from   Parliament   and   the   government,
seemingto develop into a personal feud between Burke and
Hastings, who gained increasing popular sympathy.

In   the autumn of 1795 when the trial of Hastings began,
Burke became involved in the constitutional crisis brought
about by George III's illness. Since the Prince of Wales was
believed to be favourable towards the opposition, Fox and
Burke insisted that Parliament should recognize that he had
the hereditary right to be appointed Regent immediately with
complete royal authority. Pitt, however,   believed that the
Prince had no such exclusive claim to exercise the executive
power on behalf of the King and held that Parliament was
entitled to make such provision as it thought proper to
enable the country to be governed during the monarch's
incapacity. The opposition was again unable to benefit from
this episode, despite Burke's violent speeches in Parliament
against Pitt. The King began to get better, and in March 1789
his recovery was officially announced, which put an immediate
end to the proceedings. During that time Burke supported
William Wilberforce in advocating the abolition of the slave
trade.

Though he at first reacted mildly to the storming of the Bastille in Paris in 1789, he spoke against the French Revolution in Parliament the next year and later published his Reflections on the Revolution in France, which led to his break with Fox, Sheridan and the majority of the members of the opposition. This brought him both approval and criticism. He replied the next year with the Appeal from the New to the Old Whigs, and he continued to attack the Revolution in 1791 with his Letter to a Member of the National Assembly.

He took a decreasing part in parliamentary life during the following years, though he was active in assisting the French refugee clergy in England and voted against the removal of disabilities from Unitarians and against parliamentary reform. He advised his friends to support Pitt and his followers, continued his quarrel with the Foxites and openly joined the ministerial party in 1792. The next year, together with some forty-five other members, he reigned from the Whig Club after the passing of a motion supporting Fox. He pleaded for war against France, but when it came 1793 the opening years were marked by reverses, including the French invasion of Holland, the withdrawal of Prussia from the war with the Treaty of Basel and the declaration of hostilities against Britain by Spain. These events filled Burke with despair, but he believed the war would be a long one and must be endured to the end.

In June 1794 he resigned from Parliament. His retirement was made easier for him by the decision of the ministry to obtain for him the grant of a pension from the Crown, but the death of his only surviving son (just after his election to represent Malton in Parliament in succession to his father) broke his heart. He continued, however, to involve himself in public affairs, encouraging the foundation of Maynooth College, an Irish seminary for Roman Catholic priests, and establishing a school for the sons of French refugees at Penn in Buckinghamshire. When the Duke of Bedford spoke in the House of Lords against the grant of a pension to him, he replied in 1796 with his Letter to a Noble Lord.

He was engaged on his last written work, Letters on a Regicide Peace (in answer to a pamphlet by Lord Auckland, published with Pitt's approval, advocating peace negotiations with France), when he died in July 1797. Though Fox and others proposed that he should have a tomb in Westminster Abbey, he was buried, in accordance with his will, in Beaconsfield Parish Church in the same grave as his son and brother.

Chronology

During the first part of Burke's life, two calendars were in use in the British Isles. Until 31st. December 1751 the Julian or Old Style was the legal calendar. It was eleven days behind the Gregorian or New Style, which was used in all other countries except Russia and Turkey. In addition, the legal beginning of the year in the British Isles was 25th. March (Lady Day) and not 1st. January as in other countries. By an Act of Parliament in 1751, however, the Julian calendar was superseded by the Gregorian in the British Isles. By this Act the day following 31st. December 1751 became 1st. January 1752. In order to correct the error of eleven days in the Julian calendar, the eleven days between 2nd. and 14th. September were omitted from the calendar for that year, making the day after 2nd. September 1752 the 14th. September. The succession of days of the week remained the same.

It was a common British practice to use, especially when dating letters, both styles. Burke's date of birth would, therefore, be 1st. January 1728 (Old Style) or 12th. January 1729 (New Style). Here, and elsewhere in this book, the dates of months and years are given according to the New Style. The same applies to Burke's time at Trinity College, Dublin, which, during the eighteenth century, had its own academic year beginning on 9th. July and ending on 8th. July in the next year.

    *   *   *   *   *   *   *

<u>11th. June 1727</u>	DEATH OF GEORGE I; ACCESSION OF GEORGE II.
<u>12th. January 1729</u>	Edmund Burke born in Dublin.
<u>1735?-1740?</u>	lived mainly with maternal relations in County Cork.
26th. May 1741	sent to school at Ballitore, County Kildare.
<u>14th. April 1744</u>	entered Trinity College, Dublin.
<u>26th. May 1746</u>	became Scholar of Trinity College.

<u>23rd. April 1747</u>	enrolled at Middle Temple, London.
<u>28th. January 1748</u>	started <u>The Reformer.</u>
<u>23rd. February 1748</u>	graduated from Trinity College.
<u>18th. May 1756</u>	published <u>A Vindication of Natural Society.</u>
<u>12th. March 1757</u>	married Jane Mary Nugent.
<u>9th. February 1758</u>	first son, Richard, born.
<u>14th. December 1758</u>	second son, Christopher, born (died in infancy).
<u>25th. December 1758</u>	first meeting with Samuel Johnson.
<u>1759-1765</u>	secretary to William Gerard Hamilton.
<u>15th. May 1759</u>	first number of <u>Annual Register</u> published.
<u>25th. October 1760</u>	DEATH OF GEORGE II; ACCESSION OF GEORGE III.
<u>10th. February 1763</u>	PEACE OF PARIS.
<u>19th. April 1763</u>	received pension on Irish Establishment.
<u>10th. April 1764</u>	resigned Irish pension.
<u>23rd. March 1765</u>	STAMP ACT PASSED.
<u>13th. July 1765</u>	GRENVILLE SUCCEEDED BY ROCKINGHAM.
<u>17th. July 1765</u>	Private Secretary to Lord Rockingham.
<u>23rd.December 1765</u>	elected Member of Parliament for Wendover.
<u>17th. January 1766</u>	first spoke in Parliament, on American question.
<u>11th. March 1766</u>	STAMP ACT REPEALED; DECLARATORY ACT PASSED.
<u>2nd. August 1766</u>	GRAFTON-CHATHAM MINISTRY SUCCEEDED ROCKINGHAM.
<u>4th. August 1766</u>	published <u>A Short Account of a Late Short Administration</u>.
<u>17th. January 1767</u>	received freedom of City of Dublin.
<u>28th. January 1770</u>	GRAFTON RESIGNED; SUCCEEDED BY NORTH.
<u>5th. March 1770</u>	BOSTON MASSACRE.

23rd. April 1770	published <u>Thoughts on the Present Discontents</u>.
21st. December 1770	appointed Agent to the General Assembly of New York.
12th. January - 1st. March 1773	visited France with son Richard.
16th. December 1773	BOSTON TEA PARTY.
31st. March 1774	BOSTON PORT ACT.
11th. October 1774	elected Member of Parliament for Bristol.
10th. January 1775	published <u>Speech on American Taxation</u>.
19th. April 1775	BATTLE OF LEXINGTON.
22nd. May 1775	published <u>Speech on American Conciliation</u>.
4th. July 1776	AMERICAN DECLARATION OF INDEPENDENCE.
8th. May 1777	published <u>Letter to the Sheriffs of Bristol</u>.
17th. October 1777	SURRENDER OF GENERAL BURGOYNE AT SARATOGA.
7th.December 1780	elected Member of Parliament for Malton.
19th. October 1781	SURRENDER OF LORD CORNWALLIS AT YORKTOWN.
19th. March 1782	LORD NORTH RESIGNED; SUCCEEDED BY ROCKINGHAM.
24th. March 1782	Paymaster-General of the Forces.
27th. March 1782	sworn to the Privy Council.
1st. July 1782	ROCKINGHAM DIED; SUCCEEDED BY SHELBURNE.
10th. July 1782	resigned from office.
8th. April 1783	Paymaster-General of the Forces.
24th. April 1783	SHELBURNE RESIGNED; SUCCEEDED BY PORTLAND (FOX-NORTH COALITION MINISTRY).
25th. June 1783	presented <u>Ninth Report of the Select Committee</u>.
3rd. September 1783	PEACE OF VERSAILLES.

15th. November 1783	elected Rector of Glasgow University.
19th. December 1783	COALITION DISMISSED; WILLIAM PITT'S MINISTRY FORMED.
10th. May 1787	COMMONS VOTED FORMAL IMPEACHMENT OF WARREN HASTINGS.
13th. February 1788	OPENING OF HASTING'S TRIAL.
5th. May 1789	FRENCH STATES-GENERAL MET.
17th. June 1789	FRENCH NATIONAL ASSEMBLY FORMED.
14th. July 1789	FALL OF THE BASTILLE.
4th. November 1789	RICHARD PRICE'S SERMON TO THE LONDON REVOLUTION SOCIETY AT THE OLD JEWRY MEETING HOUSE, LONDON.
8th. February 1790	speech in Parliament making his first public attack on French Revolution.
9th. February 1790	first disagreement (in Parliament) with Fox over French Revolution.
12th. July 1790	CIVIL CONSTITUTION OF FRENCH CLERGY DECREED
1st. November 1790	published Reflections on the Revolution in France.
6th. May 1791	speech in Parliament ending his friendship with Fox.
21st. May 1791	published Letter to a Member of the National Assembly.
3rd. August 1791	published An Appeal from the New to the Old Whigs.
18th.February 1792	published Letter to Sir Hercules Langrishe.
10th. August 1792	IMPRISONMENT OF FRENCH ROYAL FAMILY.
20th. September 1792	CONVENTION REPLACED NATIONAL ASSEMBLY.
22nd. September 1792	FRENCH REPUBLIC PROCLAIMED.
16th. November 1792	FRANCE OPENED RIVER SCHELDT.
1st. December 1792	BRITISH MILITIA MOBILIZED.
21st. January 1793	LOUIS XVI EXECUTED.
1st. February 1793	FRANCE DECLARED WAR ON BRITAIN.

<u>13th. February 1793</u>	FIRST COALITION FORMED.
<u>28th. February 1793</u>	resigned from the Whig Club.
<u>16th. October 1793</u>	MARIE ANTOINETTE EXECUTED.
<u>21st. June 1794</u>	resigned from Parliament.
<u>17th. July 1794</u>	Richard Burke elected M.P. for Malton.
<u>2nd. August 1794</u>	death of Richard Burke.
<u>19th. January 1795</u>	FRENCH CONQUEST OF HOLLAND.
<u>5th. April 1795</u>	TREATY OF BASEL.
<u>23rd. April 1795</u>	ACQUITTAL OF HASTINGS.
<u>22nd. September 1795</u>	received pension from Crown.
<u>24th. February 1796</u>	published <u>Letter to a Noble Lord</u>.
<u>5th. October 1796</u>	SPAIN DECLARED WAR ON BRITAIN.
<u>20th. October 1796</u>	published <u>Two Letters on a Regicide Peace</u>.
<u>9th. July 1797</u>	died.
<u>15th. July 1797</u>	buried in Beaconsfield Parish Church.
<u>1798</u>	death of William Burke.
<u>1812</u>	death of Jane Burke.

Manuscript and Archival Resources

LIBRARIES AND COLLECTIONS

Though much appears to have been destroyed during his lifetime and shortly afterwards, a great amount of material about Burke has survived, but it is now dispersed. The most important collections are indicated below by an asterisk.

GREAT BRITAIN AND IRELAND

1. National Register of Archives.
   The National Register of Archives, Quality House, Quality Court, Chancery Lane, London WC2A 1HP, has comprehensive catalogues of many of the collections of non-governmental records in the possession of British archives and libraries, as well as some American ones, and also information about conditions of access to collections in private ownership. Where it has catalogued a collection, the reference is given below in square brackets after the letters SA. See also nos. 110, 111, 113.
   In addition, a microfiche index, providing in some instances more information, but not yet mentioning all the relevant collections, has been produced by Chadwyck-Healey Ltd. of Cambridge under the title of A National Inventory of Documentary Sources in the United Kingdom. It is available in some research libraries of the United States of America.

2. Fitzwilliam MSS (Sheffield).*
   The largest number of Burke's private papers (1744–1797) are to be found in this collection. Having been formerly kept at Wentworth Woodhouse in Yorkshire, it used to be known as the 'Wentworth Woodhouse MSS.' It is now deposited with the Sheffield Central City Library, Surrey Street, Sheffield S1 1XZ. [NRA 1083 Wentworth-Fitzwilliam]. See also, HMC, Papers of British Politicians 1782-1900 (1989).

3. Fitzwilliam MSS (Sheffield), New York Letter Book.
   A folio-size notebook in which Burke made copies of the letters written by him when Agent for the General Assembly of the Province of New York from 1771 to 1775.

4. Fitzwilliam MSS (Northamptonshire).*
   This collection of thirty-six bundles, comprising about a

fifth of the main collection of Burke's papers (c1760-1797), came into the possession of the fourth Earl Fitzwilliam as the last survivor among Burke's literary executors. It was formerly kept at Milton near Peterborough and was known as the 'Milton MSS.' It is now deposited with the Northamptonshire Record Office, Lamport Hall, Northamptonshire. [NRA 4120]. See also HMC, op. cit.

5. Macpherson MSS.
    Macpherson papers in the Library of the School of Oriental and African Studies, University of London, Malet Street, London WC1.

6. O'Hara MSS.*
    Over 200 letters (1759-1776) of William, Edmund and Richard Burke to Charles O'Hara, Irish M.P., formerly in the possession of Donald F. O'Hara, Esq., and now deposited with the National Library of Ireland, Kildare Street, Dublin 2. MSS 16886-16887. Also fifty items of miscellaneous correspondence and papers (1759-1793), MS 5923.

7. Portland MSS.*
    Thirty-five letters (1766-1795) to the Duke of Portland, which are now deposited with the Library of the University of Nottingham, Manuscripts Department, University Park, Nottingham. [NRA 7628 Cavendish-Bentinck (PWF 2067-2108).

8. Dartmouth MSS.
    Manuscripts belonging to the Earl of Dartmouth, which are now deposited with the William Salt Library, Eastgate Street, Stafford.

9. Glynn MSS.
    Manuscripts of the family of Serjeant John Glynn, M.P. for Middlesex, belonging to Lt. D.H.J. Glynn, R.N., Cannon Cottage, Upton Road, Chichester, West Sussex.

10. Billitore MSS.
    A collection formerly owned by Mrs. M.R. Backhouse, when they were microfilmed. A film of all the collection is in the National Library of Ireland, and one reel, containing Burke's letters, is in the Central City Library, Manchester.

11. Verney MSS.
    Manuscripts belonging to R.B. Verney, Esq., Claydon House, Bletchley, Buckinghamshire.

12. Champion Letter-Books.
    A collection of the notebooks of Richard Champion, a Bristol merchant and china manufacturer, containing a transcription of his correspondence. A single notebook, formerly part of the collection, is now in the New York Public Library. The main body of the notebooks is in the possession of Miss Phyllis Rawlins, Denbigh, Wales.

13. Bristol Central Library.*
    Three bound folio volumes in which are pasted various election broadsides, handbills and addresses. The volumes are separately identified as:

Br 1. 'Bristol Elections 1774-1790.' Accession B6979.
Probably the collection of Thomas Garrard.
Br 2. 'Election Addresses, Squibs, etc.' Accession 7954.
Tenth volume of the C.T. Jefferies collection.
Br 3. 'Bristol Election 1774.' Accession 18197.
The collection of G.E. Weare.

14. Bristol Archives
    Chamberlain's Letter-Book and the Town Clerk's Letter-
Book and miscellaneous letters (1759-1778) in the Bristol
Record Offices, Council House, College Green, Bristol 1.

15. British Library, Great Russell Street, London WC 1B
    3DG.*
    Correspondence (1790-1795) with Lord Grenville , Add MS
69038.
    Correspondence (1793-1797) with William Windham M.P. Add
MS37843.
    Report of Committee of Secrecy, (1781), MS notes by
Burke.
T. Pownall, Administration of the Colonies (1768), MS notes
by Burke.

16. Bodleian Library, Oxford OX1 3BG.*
    Letters (1788-1797) from French Laurence, civil lawyer
and friend of Burke, MS Eng lett d 5.

17. Cambridge University Library, West Street, Cambridge.
    Extracts and copies of letters to and from Burke, Add.
MSS. 93-113, 115-139, 180-198, 130-146, 212-228, 256-310,
945, 1189, 1402, 1415, 1480, 1487, 1490, 1494, 1782,
1843,4898, 4965, 4967, 6958; H 36-49, 48-78, 280-308.
    'Thoughts on the Present Position of Affairs in Europe,'
Add. MSS. 6958 (1189).

18. Centre for Kentish Studies
    Letters (1791) to William Pitt [NRA 25095 Stanhope
(U1590/S5/01/9)]. Kent Archive Office, County Hall,
Maidstone, Kent ME14 1XQ.

19. Devon Record Office, Castle Street, Exeter EX4 3PQ.
    Correspondence (1790-1795) with Lord Sidmouth [NRA 8747
Addington].

20. Hertfordshire Record Office
    Correspondence (1771-1790) with William Baker M.P. [NRA
18350 Baker].

21. House of Lords Library.

22. Hull Trinity House.
    Trinity House, Trinity House Lane, Hull.

23. India Library, London.*
    Madras Select Committee Proceedings, Range D, vol. XXVII;
twenty-seven letters (1777-1794) to Sir Philip Francis, MSS
Eur F 6. Oriental and India Office Collections, Orbit House,
Blackfriars Road, London SE1 8NG.

24. Langdale MSS.
   Manuscripts belonging to the Countess Fitzwilliam, now
deposited in the East Riding County Record Office, County
Hall, Beverley.

25. Murray Papers.
   A collection of transcripts of Burke's letters made by
Canon Robert Murray when proposing to make a new edition of
the correspondence. On Canon Murray's death, it was first
deposited with the Bodleian Library, but has now been moved
to the Sheffield City Libraries.

26. National Library of Scotland.
   Ten letters (1783-1791) to Henry Dundas, M.P. for
Yorkshire, written 1st. March 1783, 1st., 4th., 5th., 14th.
April 1787, 11th. October 1787 - MS 16, Department of
Manuscripts, George IV Bridge, Edinburgh 1. The letter of
9th. December 1787 was given by Lord Curzon to the Victoria
Municipal Hall, Calcutta, India.

27. North Yorkshire County Record Office.
   Correspondence with the Revd. Christopher Wyvill. [NRA
13480 Wyvill (7/2)].

28. John Rylands Library, University of Manchester, Oxford
Road, Manchester M13 9PD.

29. Northumberland County Record Office, Melton Park, North
Gosforth, Newcastle-on-Tyne.

30. Public Record Office of Northern Ireland, 66 Balmoral
Avenue, Belfast BT9 6NY.

31. Ramsden MSS.
   Manuscripts owned by Sir William Pennington Ramsden, now
deposited with the Central Library, Leeds 1.

32. Rockingham MSS.
   Letters and papers of the second Marquis of Rockingham,
now deposited with the Sheffield City Libraries.

33. Society of Merchant Venturers, Merchants Hall, The
Promenade, Clifton, Bristol 8.

34. Suffolk Record Office, Ipswich Branch, County Hall. St.
Helen's Street, Ipswich IP4 2JS.

35. Trinity College Library, Dublin University, College
Street, Dublin 2.

36. Victoria and Albert Museum, Cromwell Road, South
Kensington, London SW7 2RL.

37. Public Record Office, Ruskin Avenue, Kew, Richmond,
Surrey TW9 4DU.

UNITED STATES OF AMERICA

38. Osborn MSS.*
    The James Marshall and Marie-Louise Osborn Collection of
correspondence and papers, now deposited with the Beinecke
Library, Yale University, Connecticut. [NRA 18661 Osborn
collection].

39. Harvard University.
    Twenty items of miscellaneous correspondence and papers,
NUC MS 81-455; 'Observations on the Conduct of the Minority'
(1 vol.) The Houghton Library, Harvard University, Cambridge
38, Massachusetts. [NRA 20129 Harvard Univ MSS (fms Eng
878)]. See also, HMC, op.cit.

40. Little MSS.
    Manuscripts owned by the late Professor D.M. Little of
Harvard University.

41. Hyde Collection.
    Manuscripts belonging to Mrs. Donald Hyde, Four Oaks
Farm, Somerville , New Jersey.

42. American Antiquarian Society.

43. Boston Athenaeum.

44. American Philosophical Society, 105 South 5th. Street,
Philadelphia 6, Pennsylvania.

45. Boston Public Library.

46. William L. Clements Library, Ann Arbor, Michigan.

47. The Folger Shakespeare Library, Washington 3, D.C.

48. Columbia University

49. Lehigh University.

50. Library of Congress.

51. Newberry Library.

52. Northwestern University.

53. New York Historical Society, 170 Central Park West, New
York 24, New York.
    Henry W. and Albert A. Berg Collection.

54. New York Public Library, Fifth Avenue and 42nd. Street,
New York 18, New York.

55. Oberlin College.

56. Princeton University.

57. Philadelphia Free Library.

58. Philadelphia Library Company.

59. The Pierpont Morgan Library, 33 East 36th. Street, New York 16, New York.

60. University of Alabama.

61. University of Chicago.

62. University of Illinois.

63. University of Iowa.

64. University of Michigan.

65. University of Rochester.

66. Charles Patterson Van Pelt Library, University of Pennsylvania.

67. University of Texas.

68. Washington and Jefferson College.

69. Yale University.

ELSEWHERE

70. Haus-, Hof- und Staatsarchiv, Minoritenplatz 1, Vienna.

71. Les Fontaines, 60500 Chantilly, France.

72. Bibliotheque Nationale, Paris.

73. Madras Record Office, Egmore, Madras 8.

74. Koninklijke Biblioyheke, Lange Voorhout 34, The Hague.

75. Archivio Segreto Vaticano, Rome.
    Material also on microfilm in the National Library of Ireland.

CATALOGUES AND GUIDES

British Library
76. Catalogue of Additions to Manuscripts in the British Museum (1836-   ).
77. T.C. Skeat, The Catalogues of the Manuscript Collections (revised ed., 1970).
78. British Library Journal (Spring, 1975-).
    A twice-yearly periodical including information about new accessions (superseding British Museum Quarterly).

Bodleian Library, Oxford
79. F. Madan, H.H.E. Craster, N. Denholm-Young & R.W. Hunt, A Summary Catalogue of the Western Manuscripts in the Bodleian Library at Oxford (7 vols. in 8; only lists accessions to 1915).

80. Bodleian Library Record.
    Twice-yearly; includes notes on new accessions.

Cambridge University Library
81. Summary Guide to Accessions of Western Manuscripts
    (Other than Medieval) since 1867 (1966). The original
    Catalogue of the Manuscripts (5 vols. & Index) was
    published during 1856-1867.

National Library of Scotland
82. Catalogue of Manuscripts (4 vols. published 1938-1971).
83. Accessions of Manuscripts.
    Five-yearly; succeeded the Annual Report in 1959.

84. Philip Hepworth (ed.), Select Biographical Sources:
    The Library Association Manuscripts Survey (Library
    Association, 1971).

85. G.H. Martin & P. Spufford (eds.), The Records of the
    Nation (The Boydell Press, The British Record Society,
    1990).

86. Philip M. Hamer (ed.), A Guide to Archives and
    Manuscripts in the United States (Yale University
    Press, New Haven).

87. National Union Catalog of Manuscipt Collections,
    Library of Congress, Washington, D.C.

88. The R.B. Adam Library Relating to Dr. Samuel Johnson
    and his Era (4 vols., Privately Printed, 1929-1930).
    Volume I has a portion separately paged and en-
    titled 'Letters of Edmund Burke.'

89. C. C. Abbott (ed.), Catalogue of Papers Found at
    Fettercairn House (OUP, 1936).

90. Collections of the South Carolina Historical Society (2
    vols., Charleston, S.C., 1857-1858).

91. Henry W. Aldred, The Suffolk Records (1888)

92. S. Arthur Strong (ed.), A Catalogue of Letters and
    Other Documents Exhibited in the Library at Welbeck
    (1903).

93. Catalogue of the Library, Engravings and Autographs of
    Mrs. L.A. Evans. Sold by Messrs. Bruton, Knowles & Co.,
    (Gloucester, 1904).

THE HISTORICAL MANUSCRIPTS COMMISSION.

This Royal Commission was established in 1869 for locating
and publishing manuscripts of instiutions and private
families. It has published a series of printed Reports and
Appendices, which contain both summary descriptions of the
archives of noble families, private persons and ancient
institutions, as well as detailed calendars of sections of
these. Those relevant to Burke are:

94. HMC. (American MSS).
    Historical Manuscripts Commission Report on American
    Manuscripts in the Royal Institute of Great Britain,
    (4 vols., HMSO, 1904-1909).

95. HMC. (Beaufort, Donoughmore, etc. MSS).
    Historical Manuscripts Commission, Twelfth Report,
    Appendix 9 (HMSO, 1891).

96. HMC. (Charlemont MSS).
    Historical Manuscripts Commission, Twelfth Report,
    Appendix 10 (HMSO, 2 vols., 1891).

97. HMC. (Charlemont MSS).
    Historical Manuscripts Commission, Thirteenth Report,
    Appendix 8 (HMSO, 1894).

98. HMC. (Dartmouth MSS).
    Historical Manuscripts Commission, Fourteenth Report,
    Appendix 10 (HMSO, 1887-1895).

99. HMC. (Rutland MSS).
    Historical Manuscripts Commission, Fourteenth Report,
    Appendix 1 (HMSO, 1894).

100. HMC. (Kenyon MSS).
    Historical Manuscripts Commission, Fourteenth Report,
    Appendix 4 (HMSO, 1894),

101. HMC. (Lansdown MSS).
    Historical Manuscripts Commission, Third Report.

102. HMC. (Underwood MSS).
    Historical Manuscripts Commission, Tenth Report,
    Appendix 1 [Charles Fleetwood Weston Underwood MSS],
    (HMSO, 1885).

103. HMC. (Fortescue MSS).
    Historical Manuscripts Commission, Thirteenth Report,
    Appendix 3 (HMSO, 1892).

104. HMC .(Carlisle MSS).
    Historical Manuscripts Commission, Fifteenth Report,
    Appendix 6 (HMSO, 1897).

105. J. Redington (ed.), Calendar of Home Office Papers of
    the Reign of George III (HMSO, 1878).

In addition the Commission is now publishing a series of
Guides to Sources for British History. Most useful for Burke
is:

106. Papers of British Politicians 1782-1900 (HMSO,
    1989).

Also of value in this series is:

107. Guide to the Location of Collections Described in the
    Reports and Calendar Series (HMSO, 1982)

Other relevant publications of the Commission are:

108. Manuscripts and Men (HMSO, 1969).
    A definitive illustrated catalogue for the Commission's
centenary year exhibition at the National Portrait Gallery
in 1969.

109. J.D. Cantwell, The Public Record Office 1838-1958
    (HMSO, 1991).

110. Record Repositories in Great Britain (HMSO).
    The basic directry of repositories revised every few
years.

111. Bulletin of the National Register of Archives
    (HMSO, 1948-1967).

112. Report of the Secretary to the Commissioners (HMSO,
    1968-).

113. Accessions to Repositories and Reports Added to the
    National Register of Archives (HMSO).
    Annual reports of major accessions received by principal
repositories in the year prior to publication.

CONTEMPORARY NEWSPAPERS AND JOURNALS.

114. F. B. Kaye, A Census of British Newspapers and
    Periodicals 1620-1800 (University of North Carolina
    Press, 1927).

115. R. Fox Bourne, English Newspapers (2 vols., 1887).

116. A. Aspinall, Politics and the Press, 1780-1850 (Home &
    Van Thal, 1949).

117. Lucyle T. Werkmeister, The London Daily Press, 1772-
    1792 (Lincoln, Nebraska, 1963).

118. Lucyle T. Werkmeister, A Newspaper History of England,
    1772-1793 (Lincoln, Nebraska, 1967).

119. W.D.Bowman, The Story of the Times (Routledge, 1931).

120. Robert L. Haig, The Gazeteer: A Study in the Eighteenth
    Century English Newspaper (Carbondale, 1960).

121. I.S. Asquith, 'James Perry and the Morning Chronicle'
    (London University Ph.D. dissertation, 1963).

*   *   *   *   *

122. Adam's Weekly Courant.

123. Analytical Review.

124. Bristol Gazette and Public Advertiser.

125. Bristol Journal.

126. The Briton.

127. Critical Review.

128. Daily Advertiser.

129. The Diary: or, Woodfall's Register,

130. Edinburgh Herald.

131. Edinburgh Review,

132. English Review

133. Faulkner's Dublin Journal.

134. Fortnightly Review.

135. The Gazeteer and New Daily Advertiser.

136. Gentleman's Magazine.

137. London Chronicle.

138. Lloyd's Evening Post.

139. London Evening Post.

140. London Gazette.

141. The Meddler (Dublin).

142. Morning Chronicle.

143. Morning Post.

144. St. James's Chronicle.

145. The Times (named The Daily Universal Register, 1785–1788).

146. The True Briton.

147. The World.

Published Resources

The earliest life of Burke by Charles McCormick (no. 157) was largely a party-inspired attack on him by a Foxite Whig. It was soon answered by the better work of Robert Bisset (no. 159), which contains some useful information and anecdotes. Meanwhile, C.H. Wilson's Beauties of Burke (no. 158), which contains both a memoir and extracts from his works, had appeared, and it was used considerably by James Prior in his Life of Burke (no. 160), the first comprehensive biography of him. Despite its excessive partiality for its subject and serious ill-arrangement, it remains the most reliable and factual of the nineteenth-century biographies and has been relied upon in varying degrees by subsequent biographers, together with Thomas Macknight (no. 163) who, though also badly-arranged, as well as being prolix and uncritical, did have some new miscellaneous material.

All these older writers are now out of date in their general political interpretation of Burke and also have suffered from the limitation of material that could be used by them through the long unavailability to scholars (with few exceptions) of the large collection of Burke's correspondence, which was denied to the public for nearly a hundred and fifty years. This came into the possession of Burke's literary executors, Dr. French Laurence (1757-1809), a lawyer and Member of Parliament, and Dr. Walker King (1751-1827), Bishop of Rochester. They intended to produce a biography of Burke and an edition of his letters, but died without doing this. Through the influence of Mrs. Burke, all the material then came into the possession of his friend and patron, William Wentworth Fitzwilliam, second Earl Fitzwilliam, and after his death it was stored in the muniment room of Wentworth Woodhouse, the family mansion in Yorkshire, by his descendants, who refused to allow them to be examined, even by the Historical Manuscripts Commission.

In 1949, however, the ninth Earl Fitzwilliam transferred these papers to Sheffield (see no. 2). At the same time Captain Thomas W. Fitzwilliam, now the tenth Earl Fitzwilliam, placed the next largest collection of Burke manuscripts with the Northamptonshire Record Office (see no. 4); and the papers of the second Marquis of Rockingham and the fourth Earl Fitzwilliam were deposited at Sheffield (see no. 32). These changes, followed by the comprehensive publication of Burke's correspondence and of the still-appearing collection of his letters and speeches (see nos.424, 353), have started to improve the situation.

Sir Philip Magnus (see. no. 185) wrote after being granted access to the Fitzwilliam collections, but his book was not planned as an exhaustive and final biography and did not add much more to knowledge about Burke than any writer since Prior. R.H. Murray (see no. 183) wrote comprehensively, but without access to the new material. Stanley Ayling's biography (see no. 227) is the first to be based upon the full extant correspondence, which gives it an inevitable advantage over its predecessors.

At the same time, scholarly and critical interest in Burke's philosophical and political thought and influence has steadily increased, particularly during the last forty years. In 1959 some American scholars, with the intention of promoting scholarly discussion of Burke's work, established the Burke Newsletter, which has continued with title changes to indicate its broadening aims (see no. 676).

Carl B. Cone's Burke and the Nature of Politics (see no. 208) is the most substantial modern study of Burke's thought and work and is supplemented by Frank O'Gorman's Edmund Burke, His Political Philosophy (see no. 216) and Isaac Kramnick's lively, contentious psychobiography, The Rage of Edmund Burke, Portrait of an Ambivalent Conservative (see no. 220).

In addition, since the last war there has been a growth in the 'New Conservative' interpretation of Burke's philosophy with its emphasis on Natural Law, although this has been more marked in America than in England. Prominent works putting forward this approach have been Russell Kirk's The Conservative Mind from Burke to Santayana (see no. 195); Peter Stanlis's Edmund Burke and the Natural Law (see no. 209); and F. Canavan's The Political Reason of Edmund Burke (see no. 203); while it has been discussed by B.T. Wilkins's The Problem of Burke's Political Philosophy (see no. 213).

Another attitude has been to approach Burke's ideas in the context of his time and consider what he meant in expressing them. This has especially produced a growing number of specialized, concentrated studies, such as those by A.P.I. Samuels, Ernest Barker, Dixon Wecter, Thomas W. Copeland, Alfred Cobban and C.R. Ritcheson (see nos. 179, 184, 187, 194, 201, 219).

BIBLIOGRAPHIES [See also No. 352]

148. S. Pargellis & P.J. Medley, Bibliography of British History: The Eighteenth Century, 1714-1789 (OUP, 1951).

149. Donald C. Bryant, 'Report on Burke Studies,' Quarterly Journal of Speech, vol. IVL, no. 4 (1958), pp. 434-442.

150. Thomas W. Copeland, 'The Reputation of Edmund Burke,' Journal of British Studies, vol. I, no. 2 (1962), pp. 78-90.

151. Donald C. Bryant, 'Edmund Burke: A Generation of Scholarship and Discovery,' Journal of British Studies, vol. II, no. 1 (1962), pp. 91-114.

152. P.J. Stanlis, 'Edmund Burke in the Twentieth Century,' Bucknell Review, vol. XII, no. 2 (1964), pp. 65-89. [Reprinted in no. 212 below].

153. W.D. Love, '"Meaning" in the Conflicting Interpretations of Burke,' Burke Newsletter, vol. VII, no. 2 (1966), pp. 526-538. [Reprinted in no. 212 below].

154. C.I. Gandy, 'A Bibliographical Survey of Writings on Edmund Burke, 1945 - 1975,' British Studies Monitor, vol. VIII, no. 1 (1978), pp. 3-21.

155. Gayle Trusdel Pendleton, 'Towards a Bibliography of the Reflections and Rights of Man Controversy,' Bulletin of Research in the Humanities, vol. LXXXV, no. 1 (1982), p. 68.

156. C.I. Gandy & P.J. Stanlis, Edmund Burke: A Bibliography of Secondary Studies to 1982 (Garland, New York, 1983).

BIOGRAPHIES AND STUDIES

157. Charles M'Cormick, Memoirs of Edmund Burke (London, 1797).

158. C. H. Wilson (ed.), The Beauties of the Late Right Hon. Edmund Burke (2 vols., 1798).

159. Robert Bisset, Life of Edmund Burke (2 vols., 2nd. ed., George Cawthorn, 1800).

160. Sir James Prior, The Life of the Right Honourable Edmund Burke (1st. ed 1824; 5th. ed., Bell, 1882).

161. George Croly, A Memoir of the Political Life of Edmund Burke, with Extracts from His Writings (Blackwood, Edinburgh, 1840).

162. Peter Burke, The Public and Domestic Life of the Right Honourable Edmund Burke (Ingram, Cooke, 1853).

163. Thomas MacKnight, History of the Life and Times of Edmund Burke (3 vols., London 1858-1860).

164. H.C. van Schaack, Henry Cruger: The Colleague of Edmund Burke in the British Parliament (New York, 1859).

165. John, Viscount Morley, Edmund Burke, An Historical Study (Macmillan, 1867).

166. Sir Leslie Stephen, History of English Thought in the Eighteenth Century (Smith, Elder & Co., 2 vols., 1872). [Vol. II].

167. Sir N.W. Wraxall, Historical Memoirs of My Own Time (5 vols, Bickers & Son, 1884).

168. E.A. Pankhurst, Edmund Burke, A Study of Life and Character (Hamilton, Adams & Co., 1886).

169. G.E. Weare, Edmund Burke's Connection with Bristol from 1774 till 1780 with a Prefatory Memoir of Burke (W. Bennett, Bristol, 1894).

170. John, Viscount Morley, Burke (Macmillan, 1893).

171. James A. Robertson, Lectures on the Life, Writings and Times of Edmund Burke (1896).

172. Benjamin F. Brooke, Edmund Burke, A Literary Essay (Arnold, Leeds, 1896).

173. T.D. Pillans, Edmund Burke, Apostle of Justice and Liberty (Watts & Co., 1905).

174. J. McCunn, The Political Philosophy of Burke (Edward Arnold, 1913).

175. Geoffrey G. Butler, The Tory Tradition: Bolingbroke, Burke, Disraeli, Salisbury (John Murray, 1914).

176. H.N. Brailsford, Shelley, Godwin and their Circle (OUP, 2nd. ed., 1951). [Chap. I].

177. Frieda Braune, Edmund Burke in Deutschland (Heidelburger Abhandlunger zur Mittleren and Neuren Geschichte, 1917).

178. Harold J.Laski, Political Thought from Locke to Bentham (1920). [Chap. VI].

179. Arthur P.I. Samuels, The Early Life, Correspondence and Writings of the Rt. Hon. Edmund Burke (CUP, 1923).

180. Richmond Lennox, Edmund Burke und sein Politisches Arbeitsfeld in den Jahren 1760 bis 1790 (Munich & Berlin 1923).

181. William O'Brien, Edmund Burke as an Irishman (2nd, ed., M.H. Gill & Son, Dublin, 1926).

182. Bertram Newman, Edmund Burke (Bell, 1927).

183. Robert Murray, Edmund Burke (OUP, 1931).

184. Ernest Barker, Burke and Bristol, A Study of the Relations between Burke and his Constituency during the Years 1774-1780 (J.W. Arrowsmith, Bristol, 1931).

185. Sir Philip Magnus, Edmund Burke, A Life (John Murray 1939).

186. Donald Cross Bryant, Edmund Burke and his Literary Friends (Washington University Studies, New Series: Language and Literature, no. 9, Washington University Press, St. Louis Mo., 1939).

187. Dixon Wecter, Edmund Burke and His Kinsmen: A Study of the Statesman's Integrity and Private Relationships (University of Colorado Studies, Series B, vol. I. no. 1, Boulder, 1939).

188. Sir Ernest Barker, 'Edmund Burke et la Revolution francaise,' La Revolution de 1789 et la Pensee Moderne Moderne (La Revue Philosophique, Presses Universitaires, 1940).

189. M. Osborn, Rousseau and Burke: A Study of the Idea of Liberty in Eighteenth-Century Thought (OUP, 1940).

190. G. Sampson, The Concise Cambridge History of English Literature (CUP, 1941) [Chapter XI].

191. Beni Prasad, Edmund Burke on Indian Governance (University of Allahabad Studies, Political Section, Allahabad: Senate House, 1944).

192. D. C. Bryant, 'Edmund Burke and James Barry,' Elizabethan Studies and Other Essays in Honor of George F. Reynolds (University of Colorado Studies in the Humanities), vol. II, no. 4, (1945), pp. 244-253.

193. H. J. Laski, Edmund Burke (Trinity College Dublin Historical Society, 1947).

194. E. E. Reynolds, Edmund Burke: Christian Statesman (Student Christian Movement Press, 1948).

195. Thomas W. Copeland, Our Eminent Friend Edmund Burke, Six Essays (Jonathan Cape, 1950).

196. R. Kirk, The Conservative Mind from Burke to Santayana (Regnery, Chicago, Ill., 1953).

197. C. Parkin, The Moral Basis of Burke's Political Thought: The Age of American Revolution (University of Kentucky Press, 1956).

198. Ross J. Hoffman, Edmund Burke, New York Agent (American Philosophical Society, Philadelphia, 1956).

199. C. B. Cone, Burke and the Nature of Politics (University of Kentucky Press, 2 vols., 1957-1964).

200. Peter J. Stanlis, Edmund Burke and the Natural Law (University of Michigan Press, 1959).

201. A. Cobban, Edmund Burke and the Revolt against the Eighteenth Century (Macmillan, 2nd. ed.,1960).

202. Thomas H.D. Mahoney, Edmund Burke and Ireland (Harvard University Press, Cambridge, Mass., 1960).

203. Francis P. Canavan, The Political Reason of Edmund Burke (Duke University Press, Durham, NC, 1960).

204. P.I. Underdown, Bristol and Burke (Bristol Branch of the Historical Association, 1961).

205. James Boulton, The Language of Politics in the Age of Wilkes and Burke (Routledge and Kegan Paul, 1963).

206. C. P. Courtney, Montesquieu and Burke (Basil Blackwell, Oxford, 1963).

207. R.R. Fennessy, Burke, Paine and the Rights of Man: A Difference of Political Opinion (Nijhoff, The Hague, 1963.

208. Carl B. Cone, Burke and the Nature of Politics; The Age of the French Revolution (University of Kentucky Press, 1964).

209. P.J. Stanlis, The Relevance of Edmund Burke (Kennedy, New York, 1964)

210. P. Fussell, The Rhetorical World of Augustan Humanism: Ethics and Imagery from Swift to Burke (OUP, 1965).

211. G.W. Chapman, Edmund Burke, the Practical Imagination (Harvard University Press, Cambridge, Mass., 1967).

212. P.J. Stanlis (ed.), Edmund Burke: The Enlightenment and the Modern World (University of Detroit Press, 1967).

213. B.T. Wilkins, The Problem of Burke's Political Philosophy (OUP, 1967).

214. R. Kirk, Edmund Burke: A Genius Reconsidered (Arlington House, New Rochelle, NY, 1967).

215. Michel Ganzin, La Pensée Politique d'Edmund Burke (Librairie Generale de Droit et de Jurisprudence, Paris, 1972).

216. F. O'Gorman, Edmund Burke, His Political Philosophy (Allen & Unwin, 1973).

217. David Cameron, The Social Thought of Rousseau and Burke Weidenfeld & Nicolson, 1973).

218. B.W. Hill (ed.), Edmund Burke on Government, Politics and Society (Fontana, 1975).

219. C.R. Ritcheson, Edmund Burke and the American Revolution (Leicester University Press, 1976).

220. Isaac Kramnick, The Rage of Edmund Burke: Portrait of an Ambivalent Conservative (Basic Books, New York, 1977).

221. Frederick A. Dreyer, Burke's Politics: A Study in Whig Orthodoxy (Wilfred Laurier University Press, Waterloo, Ontario, 1979).

222. M. Freeman, <u>Edmund Burke and the Critique of Political Radicalism</u> (Blackwell, Oxford, 1980).

223. C.B. Macpherson, <u>Burke</u> (OUP, 1980).

224. George Fasel, <u>Edmund Burke</u> (Twayne, Boston, Mass., 1983).

225. F.P. Lock, <u>Burke's Reflections on the Revolution in France</u> (Allen & Unwin, 1985).

226. C. Reid, <u>Edmund Burke and the Practice of Political Writing</u> (Gill & Macmillan, 1985)

227. Stanley Ayling, <u>Edmund Burke, His Life and Opinions</u> (John Murray, 1988).

228. Conor Cruse O'Brien, <u>The Great Melody: A Thematic Biography and Commented Anthology of Edmund Burke</u> (Sinclair-Stevenson, 1992).

ARTICLES AND ESSAYS

229. Henry Lord Brougham, 'Mr. Burke,' <u>Historical Sketches of Statesmen Who Flourished in the Time of George III</u> (Richard Griffin, 3 vols., 1839-1843).

230. Mrs. F. Crewe, 'Extracts from Mr. Burke's Table Talk,' <u>Miscellanies of the Philobiblion Society</u>, (vol. VII, 1862-1863).

231. Heinrich von Sybel, 'Edmund Burke und Irland,' <u>Kleine Historischen Schriften</u> (Marburg, 1869), vol. I, pp. 466-510.

232. Sir James Fitzjames Stephen, 'Four Essays on Burke,' <u>Horae Sabaticae</u>, Series III (1892). [Essays reprinted from the <u>Saturday Review</u>].

233. <u>Peptographia Dubliniensis, Memorial Discourses Preached in the Chapel of Trinity College, Dublin</u> (Dublin, 1895-1902).

234. Woodrow Wilson, 'The interpreter of English Liberty,' <u>Mere Literature and Other Essays</u> (Boston, 1896).

235. Charles Geake (ed.), 'Burke,' <u>Appreciations and Addresses Delivered by Lord Rosebery</u> (1899).

236. H.V.F. Somerset, 'Some Papers of Edmund Burke on his Pension,' <u>English Historical Review</u> (vol. XIV, 1899), pp. 110-114.

237. Sir H.J.C. Grierson, 'Edmund Burke,' <u>Cambridge History of English Literature</u> (vol. IX, 1914).

238. George Robert Stirling Taylor, 'Burke,' <u>Modern English Statesmen</u> (1920).

239. Archibald Philip Primrose, Fifth Earl of Rosebery, 'Edmund Burke,' Miscellanies Literary and Historical (2 vols., 1921).

240. L.S. Sutherland, 'Edmund Burke and the First Rockingham Ministry,' English Historical Review, vol. XLVII (1932), pp. 46-72. [Reprinted, Rosalind Mitchinson (ed.), Essays in Eighteenth-Century History (Longmans, 1966), pp. 45-71].

241. Padraic Colum, 'An Irish Constitutionalist and Irish Revolutionist, 1. - Edmund Burke. 2. - James Fintan Lalor,' Dublin Magazine, vol. IX, no. 1 (1934), pp. 57-67.

242. Donald C. Bryant, 'Edmund Burke's Opinions of Some Orators of his Day,' Quarterly Journal of Speech, vol. XX, no. 2 (April 1934), pp. 241-254. [With notes on the Members of Parliament mentioned].

243. Hano de Wet Jensen, 'Das konservative Welt-und-Staatsbild Edmund Burkes,' Anglia, vol. LVIII (1934), pp. 155-224, 225-291.

244. Mario Einaudi, 'The British Background of Burke's Political Philosophy,' Political Science Quarterly, vol. XLIX, no. 4 (December 1934), pp. 576-598.

245. Friedrich Meinecke, 'Edmund Burkes Leistung fur den Historismus,' Preussich Akademie Wissens, Sitzungs. Philos.- Hist. Klasse, vol. XIV, no 2 (Mai 1935, pp. 218-219.
[Also published in Forschungen und Fortschritte,vol. XI (1935), pp. 284-285].

246. Paul H. Emden, 'Burke,' Regency Pageant (Hodder & Stoughton, 1936).

247. A.A. Baumann, 'Burke: The Founder of Conservatism,' Personalities (Macmillan, 1936).

248. Arnold Hyde, 'Burke,' Manchester Literary Club Papers for 1935, vol. LXI (1936), pp. 20-39.

249. F.J.C. Hearnshaw, 'Burke and Sublimated Common Sense,' Some Great Political Idealists of the Christian Era (Harrap, 1937).

250. Christopher Hobhouse, 'Burke and Fox,' From Anne to Victoria: Essays by Various Hands, ed. Bonamy Dobrée (Cassell, 1937).

251. H.V.F. Somerset, 'Edmund Burke, England and the Papacy,' Dublin Review, vol. CCII (January-March 1938), pp. 138-148. [His attitude towards Roman Catholic emancipation].

252. Dixon Wecter, 'Adam Smith and Burke,' Notes and Queries, vol. CLXXXIV, no. 18 (30th. April 1938), pp. 310 - 311. [Their relationship with each other].

253. D. Wecter, 'Burke's Prospective Duel,' Ibid, vol. CLXXXIV (1938), pp. 186-7, 296-297. [With Alexander Wedderburn, later Earl of Rosslyn, in 1777].

254. D. Wecter, 'Four Letters from George Crabbe to Edmund Burke,' Review of English Studies, vol. XIV, no. 55 (July 1938), pp. 1102-1125.

255. D. Wecter, 'Two Notes on the Biography of Edmund Burke,' Notes and Queries, vol. CLXXXV, no. 24 (10th. December 1938), pp. 417-418.

256. D. Wecter, 'The Missing Years in Edmund Burke's Biography,' Publication of the Modern Languages Association of America, vol. LIII, no. 4 (December 1938), pp. 1102-1125.

257. H.V.F. Somerset, 'Edmund Burke Outside Politics,' Dublin Review, vol. CCIV (January 1939), pp. 140-146.

258. D. Wecter, 'Horace Walpole and Edmund Burke,' Modern Language Notes, vol. LIV no. 2 (February 1939), pp. 124-126. [Letter from Walpole to Burke 1777, with note].

259. Thomas W. Copeland, 'Burke and Dodsley's Annual Register, 'Publication of the Modern Languages Association of America, vol. LIV, no. 1 (March 1939), pp.223-245. [His editorship].

260. Sir Philip Magnus, 'The Finances of Edmund Burke, Unpublished Documents,' The Times Literary Supplement, no. 1944 (6th. May 1939), p. 272.

261. D. Wecter, 'Sir Joshua Reynolds and the Burkes,' Philological Quarterly, vol. XVIII, no. 3 (July 1939), pp. 301-305.

262. Ernest Barker, 'Edmund Burke et la Revolution francaise,' Revue Philosophique, vol. CXXVIII (1939), pp. 129-160.

263. D. Wecter, 'David Garrick and the Burkes,' Ibid, vol. XVIII, no. 4 (October 1939), pp. 367-380.

264. D. Wecter, 'Burke, Franklin and Samuel Petrie,' Huntingdon Library Quarterly, vol. III, no. 3 (April 1940), pp. 315-338. [Peace negotiations in 1777].

265. William Clyde Dunn, 'Adam Smith and Edmund Burke: Complementary Contemporaries', Southern Economic Journal, vol. VII (January 1941), pp. 330-346.

266. Donald C. Bryant, 'Edmund Burke's Conversation,' Studies in Speech and Drama in Honor of Alexander M. Drummund (Cornell University Press, Ithaca, N.Y., 1941), pp. 354-368.

267. P.L. Carver, 'Burke and the Totalitarian System,' Toronto University Quarterly,vol. XII, no. 1 (October 1942), pp. 32-47.

268. G.M. Young, 'Burke,' Proceedings of the British Academy, vol. XXIX (1943), p. 6.

269. Robert M. Hutchins, 'The Theory of the State: Edmund Burke,' Review of Politics, vol. V (April 1943), pp. 139-155.

270. Victor M. Hamm, 'Burke and Metaphysics, 'New Scholasticism, vol. XVIII, no. 1 (January 1944), pp. 3-18.

271. C. & D.Plimmer, 'Burke and the Abolition of Slavery,' The British Empire (BBC., 7 vols., 1945), vol. II, pp. 462-464.

272. Carl B. Cone, 'Edmund Burke the Farmer,' Agricultural History, vol. XIX, no. 1 (April 1945), pp. 65-69. [His experiments at Beaconsfield].

273. C.B. Cone, 'Pamphlet Replies to Burke's Reflections,' Southwestern Social Science Quarterly, vol. XXVI (June 1945), pp. 22-34.

274. Sir Ernest Barker, 'Burke and Bristol,' Essays on Government (OUP, 1945).

275. Hans Barth, 'Edmund Burke und die Deutsche Staatsphilosophie im Zeitalter der Romantik,' Schweizer Beitiage zur Allgemeinen Geschichte, vol. III (1945), pp. 124-157.

276. Basil Willey, 'Edmund Burke,' The Eighteenth Century Background (Chatto & Windus, 1946).

277. G.M. Young, 'Burke,' To-Day and Yesterday (Rupert Hart-Davis, 1948).

278. W.S. Maugham, 'After Reading Burke,' Cornhill Magazine (1950) p. 24.

279. A. Paul Lavack, 'Edmund Burke, His Friends and the Dawn of Irish Catholic Emancipation,' The Catholic Historical Review, vol. XXXVII (January 1952), p. 406.

280. Thomas W. Copeland, 'Burke's First Patron [William Gerard Hamilton],' History ToDay, vol. II (1952), pp. 394-399.

281. H.A. Schmitt & J.C. Weston, 'Ten Letters to Edmund Burke from the French Translator of the Reflections on the Revolution in France,' Journal of Modern History, vol. XXXIV (1952), pp. 406-423; vol. XXXV (1953), pp. 49-61.

282. Bertram D. Sarason, 'Edmund Burke and the Two Annual Registers,' Publication of the Modern Languages Association of America, vol. LXVII (1953), pp. 496-508.

283. John Gill, 'Edmund Burke,' Great Conservatives, (Conservative Political Centre, 1953).

284. Russell Kirk, 'Burke and the Philosophy of Prescription,' Journal of the History of Ideas, vol. XIV (1953), pp. 365-380.

285. James T. Boulton, 'The Reflections: Burke's Preliminary Draft and Methods of Composition,' Durham University Journal, vol. XXXXV, no. 3 (1953), pp. 114-119.

286. P.T. Underdown, 'Edmund Burke as a Member of Parliament for Bristol: A Study of his Relations with his Colleague, Henry Cruger, and with his Constituents' (Unpublished Dissertation, University of London, 1954).

287. 'I.R. Christie, 'Henry Cruger and the End of Edmund Burke's Connection with Bristol,' Transactions of the Bristol and Gloucestershire Archaeological Society, vol. LXXIV (1955), pp. 153-170.

288. A.A. Rogow, 'Burke and the American Liberal Tradition,' Antioch Review, vol. XVII, no. 2 (1950), pp. 255-265.

289. Thomas H.D. Mahoney, 'Edmund Burke 1729-1797, A Portrait and an Appraisal,' History ToDay, vol. VI (1956), pp. 727-734.

290. Bruce Mazlish, 'The Conservative Revolution of Edmund Burke,' Review of Politics (January 1958).

291. P.T. Underdown, 'Edmund Burke, the Commissary of his Bristol Constituents, 'English Historical Review, vol. LXXIII (1958), pp. 256-269.

293. P.T. Underdown, 'Burke's Bristol Friends,' Transactions of the Bristol and Gloucestershire Archaeological Society, vol. LXXXVII, (1958), pp. 127-150.

294. C.B. Macpherson, 'Burke and the New Conservatism,' Science and Society, vol. XXII, no. 3 (1958), pp. 231-239.

295. C.B. Macpherson, 'Edmund Burke,' Transactions of the Royal Society of Canada, vol. LIII, Sect. I (1959), pp. 19-26.

296. James F. Davidson, 'Natural Law and International Law in Burke,' _Review of Politics_, vol. XXI, no. 3 (1959), pp. 483-494.

297. J. Bronowski & Bruce Mazlish, 'Edmund Burke,' _The Western Intellectual Tradition_ (Hutchinson, 1960).

298. J.G.A. Pocock, 'Burke and the Ancient Constitution - A Problem in the History of Ideas,' _Historical Journal_, vol. III (1960), pp. 125-143. [Reprinted in J.G.A. Pocock, _Politics, Language and Time: Essays on Political Thought and History_ (Methuen, 1972)].

299. N.C. Phillips, 'Edmund Burke and the County Movement, 1779 - 1780,' _English Historical Review_, vol. LXXVI (1961), pp. 27-54. [Reprinted, _op. cit._, pp. 301-325.]

300. John C. Weston, Jr., 'Edmund Burke's View of History,' _Review of Politics_, vol. XXIII, no. 2 (1961), pp. 203-229.

301. John Brooke, 'Edmund Burke,' Sir Lewis Namier & John Brooke (eds.), _The History of Parliament: The House of Commons 1754-1790_ (3 vols., HMSO, 1964), vol. II, p. 153.

302. Walter D. Love, 'Edmund Burke's Idea of the Body Corporate: A Study in Imagery,' _Review of Politics_, vol. vol. XXVII, no. 2 (1965), pp. 184-197.

303. Paul Lucas, 'On Edmund Burke's Doctrine of Prescription; or, An Appeal from the New to the Old Lawyers,' _Historical Journal_, vol. XI (1968), pp. 35-63.

304. Albert Goodwin, 'The Political Genesis of Burke's _Reflections on the Revolution in France_,' _Bulletin of John Rylands Library_, vol. L, no. 2 (1968), pp. 336-364.

305. J.H. Plumb, 'Edmund Burke and his Cult,' _In the Light of History_ (Allen Lane, 1972), pp. 95-101.

306. Conor Cruse O'Brien, 'An Anti-Machiavel, Edmund Burke,' _The Suspecting Glance_ (Faber, 1972), pp. 33-49.

307. Seamus F. Deane, 'Lord Acton and Edmund Burke,' _Journal of the History of Ideas_, vol XXXIII, no. 2 (1972). pp. 325-335.

308. F. P. Canavan, 'Burke on Prescription of Government,' _Review of Politics_, vol. XXXV, no. 4 (1973), pp. 454-474.

309. P.H. Melvin, 'Burke on Theatricality and Revolution,' _Journal of the History of Ideas_, vol. XXXVI, no. 3 (1975), pp. 447-468.

310. G.S. Volkova, ['Edmund Burke as Portrayed in Anglo-American Bourgeois Historiography'], _Voprosy Istorii_, vol. II (1975), pp. 172-181.

311. Robert W. Smith, 'Edmund Burke's Negro Code,' History ToDay, vol. XXVI (1976), pp. 715-723.

312. P.J. Stanlis, 'Burke and the Utilitarians,' Studies in Burke and His Times, vol. XVIII (1977), pp. 191-198.

313. Rodney W. Kilcup, 'Burke's Historicism,' Journal of Modern History, vol. IL, no. 3 (1977). pp. 394-410.

314. J. R. Dunwiddy, 'Burke and the Utilitarians: A Rejoinder,' Ibid, vol. XIX (1978), pp. 119-126.

315. J.E. Tierney, 'Edmund Burke, John Hawkesworth, the Annual Register and the Gentleman's Magazine,' Huntingdon Library Quarterly vol. XXXXII (1978), pp. 57-72.

316. F.A. Dreyer, 'The Genesis of Burke's Reflections,' Journal of Modern History, vol. L (1978), pp. 462-479.

317. Rodney W. Kilcup, 'Reason and the Basis of Morality in Burke,' Journal of the History of Philosophy, vol XVII, no. 3 (1979), pp. 271-284.

318. R. Janes, 'At Home Abroad: Edmund Burke in India,' Bulletin of Research in the Humanities, vol. VXXXII (1979), pp. 160-174.

319. W. Vanech, 'Painful Homecoming: Reflections on Burke and India' [a reply to Professor Janes], Ibid, pp. 175-184.

320. R. Janes, 'High Flying: Edmund Burke's Eire-India' [a response to Professor Vanech], Ibid, pp. 185-189.

321. W,J. Reedy, 'Burke and Bonald: Paradigms of the Late Eighteenth Century,' Historical Reflections / Reflexions Historiques, vol. VIII/II (1981), pp. 69-93.

322. F.A. Dreyer, 'Legitimacy and Usurpation in the Thought of Edmund Burke,' Albion, vol. XII (1980), pp. 257-267.

323. A.D. Kriegel, 'Edmund Burke and the Quality of Honour,' Ibid. pp. 237-249.

324. Rod Preece, 'Edmund Burke and his European Reputation,' Eighteenth Century: Theory and Interpretation, vol. XXI, no. 3 (1980), pp. 255-273.

325. F.S. Troy, 'Edmund Burke and the Break with Tradition: History versus Psychohistory,' Massachusetts Review, vol. XXII, no. 1 (1981), pp. 93-132.

326. W. Stafford, 'Religion and the Doctrine of Nationalism in England at the Time of the French Revolution and Napoleonic Wars,' S. Mews (ed.), Religion and National Identity (Studies in Church History, vol. XVIII, Blackwell, Oxford, 1982), pp. 381-395.

327. J.G.A. Pocock, 'The Political Economy of Burke's Analysis of the French Revolution,' <u>Historical Journal</u>, vol. XXV, no. 2 (1982), pp. 331-349.

328. I. Kramnick, 'The Left and Edmund Burke,' <u>Political Theory</u>, vol. XI, no. 2 (1983), pp. 189-214.

329. David Aers, 'Coleridge and the Egg that Burke Laid: Ideological Collusion and Opposition in the 1790s,' <u>Literature and History</u>, vol. IX, no. 2 (1983), pp. 152-163.

330. E.A. Reitan, 'Edmund Burke and Economic Reform,' <u>Studies in Eighteenth-Century Culture</u>, vol. XIV (1985), pp. 129-158.

331. G. Kelly, 'Revolution, Crime and Madness: Edmund Burke and the Defense of the Gentry,' <u>Eighteenth Century Life</u>, vol. IX/I (1985), pp. 16-32.

332. D. Winch, 'The Burke-Smith Problem and Late Eighteenth-Century Political and Economic Thought,' <u>Historical Journal</u>, vol. XXVIII (1985), pp. 231-249.

333. Peter Alter, 'Edmund Burke: Reformendenken in der Epoche der Revolution,' P. Alter (ed.), <u>Geschichte des Politischen Handels</u> (Klett-Cotta, Stuttgart, 1985), pp. 70-84.

334. C. Bridge, 'Burke and the Conservative Tradition,' D. Close & C. Bridge (eds.), <u>Revolution: A History of the Idea</u> (Croom Holm, 1985).

335. R. Janes, 'Edmund Burke's Flying Leap from India into France,' <u>History of European Ideas</u>, vol. VII (1986), pp. 509-527.

336. James Conniff, 'Edmund Burke on the Coming Revolution in Ireland,' <u>Journal of the History of Ideals</u>, vol. XLVII (1986), pp. 37-59.

337. G.A. Wells, 'Burke on Ideas, Words and Imagination,' <u>British Journal for Eighteenth-Century Studies</u>, vol. IX (1986), pp. 45-51.

338. James Conniff, 'Burke on Political Economy: The Nature and Extent of State Authority,' <u>Review of Politics</u>, vol. IL (1987), pp. 490-514.

339. Jeremy Black, 'Edmund Burke: History, Politics and Polemic,' <u>History ToDay</u>, vol. XXXVII (December, 1987, pp. 42-47).

340. Maurice Crosland, 'The Image of Science as a Threat: Burke versus Priestley and the Philosophic Revolution,' <u>British Journal for the History of Science</u>, vol. XX (1987), pp. 277-307.

341. J.J. Sack, 'The Memory of Burke and the Memory of Pitt: English Conservatism Confronts its Past,' Historical Journal, vol. XXX (1987), pp. 623-640.

342. Iain Hampsher-Monk, 'Rhetoric and Opinion in the Politics of Edmund Burke,' History of Political Thought, vol. IX (1988), pp. 455-484.

343. Stephen A. Browne, 'Edmund Burke's Letter to a Noble Lord: A Textual Study in Political Philosophy and Rhetorical Action,' Communication Monographs, vol. LV (1988), pp. 215-227.

344. George C. McElroy, 'Edmund, William and Richard Burke's First Attack on Indian Misrule,1778,' Bodleian Library Record, vol. XIII (1988), pp. 52-65.

345. Roger Scruton, 'Man's Second Disobedience: A Vindication of Burke,' Ian Small & Ceri Crossley (eds.), The French Revolution and British Culture (OUP, 1989), pp. 187-222.

346. Geoffrey Carnall, 'Burke as a Modern Cicero,' G. Carnall & Colin Nicholson (eds.), The Impeachment of Warren Hastings: Papers from a Bicentenary Commemoration (Edinburgh University Press, 1989), pp. 76-90.

347. Conor Cruse O'Brien, 'Warren Hastings in Burke's Great Melody,' Ibid, pp. 58-75.

348. Gregory Claeys, 'Republicanism versus Commercial Society: Paine, Burke and the French Revolution Debate,' Society for the Study of Labour History Bulletin, vol. LIV/III (1989), pp. 4-13.

349. Suzy Halimi, 'La Notion de Progres dans Reflections on the Revolution in France d'Edmund Burke,' Etudes Anglaises, vol. XXXXII (1989), pp. 55-67.

350. Terry Eagleton, 'Aesthetics and Politics in Edmund Burke,' History Workshop, vol. XXVIII (1989), pp. 53-62.

351. Mark A. Garnett, 'Hazlitt against Burke: Radical versus Conservative,' Durham University Journal, (June 1989), pp. 229-239.

Writings by Burke

MISCELLANEOUS WORKS

352. William B. Todd, <u>A Bibliography of Edmund Burke</u> (Rupert Hart-Davis, 1964).
Extends from Burke's earliest printings in 1748 to the final issue of his collected works in 1827 and also lists works falsely assigned to Burke and imitations, parodies and imaginary literature.

*   *   *   *   *   *   *   *   *

353. P. Langford (general ed.), <u>The Writings and Speeches of Edmund Burke</u> (OUP)
A new collection of Burke's works, which is currently in course of production. So far published are:
Vol. II, P. Langford (ed.), <u>Party, Parliament and the American Crisis 1766-1774</u> (1981);
Vol. V, P. Langford (ed.), <u>India, Madras and Bengal 1774-1785</u> (1981);
Vol. VIII, L.G. Mitchell (ed.), <u>1790-1794</u> (1989).

Until it is complete, these collections of Burke's works must also be used. The fullest are nos. 355, 359, 362:

354. C.H. Wilson (ed.), <u>The Beauties of the Late Right Hon. Edmund Burke</u> (2 vols., London 1798).

355. French Laurence & Walker King, <u>The Works of Edmund Burke</u> (16 vols., London, 1803-1827).

356. George Croly, <u>A Memoir of the Political Life of Edmund Burke, with Extracts from his Writings</u> (Blackwood, Edinburgh, 1840).

357. Henry Rogers, <u>Works of Burke</u> (London, 1842).

358. Matthew Arnold (ed.), <u>Letters. Speeches and Tracts of Edmund Burke on Irish Affairs</u> (Macmillian, 1881).

359. <u>The Works of Edmund Burke</u> (6 vols., Bohn's British Classics, 6 vols,. 1854-1889).

360. Mrs. F. Crewe, 'Extracts from Mr. Burke's Table Talk,'
Miscellanies of the Philobiblion Society, vol. VII,
(1862-1863).

361. E.A. Pankhurst (ed.), The Wisdom of Burke, Selected
Extracts (1886).

362. The Writings and Speeches of Edmund Burke (12 vols.,
Little, Brown, Boston, 1901).

363. E.J. Payne (ed.), Burke's Select Works (3 vols., OUP,
1904).

364. T.D. Pillans (ed.), Edmund Burke, Selections (Wisdom of
the West Series, 1905).

365. A.J. Grieve (ed.). Reflections on the French Revolution
and Other Essays by Edmund Burke (Everyman, 1911).

366. A.P.I. Samuels, Early Life, Correspondence and Writings
of Edmund Burke (CUP, 1923).

367. Philip Magnus, Edmund Burke; Selected Prose (1948).

368. H.V.F. Somerset (ed.), A Notebook of Edmund Burke (CUP,
1957).

369. Alfred Cobban (ed.), The Debate on the French Revolution
1789-1800 (Black, 2nd. ed., 1960).

370. Conor Cruse O'Brien (ed.), Edmund Burke's Reflection on
the Revolution in France (Penguin Books, 1968).
The easiest available edition - its text based upon the
'Seventh Edition' (1790), the last revised by Burke.

371. R. A. Smith (ed.), Edmund Burke on Revolution (Harper
Rowe, New York, 1968).
An introduction and selections from Burke's writings other
than the Reflections.

372. B.W. Hill (sel. & ed.), Edmund Burke on Government,
Politics and Society (1975).

373. Marilyn Butler (ed.), Burke, Paine, Godwin and the
Revolution Controversy (CUP, 1984).

374. The Political Philosophy of Edmund Burke, compiled by
Iain Hampsher-Monk (1987).

His important published writings (in chronological order)
are:

375. Hints for an Essay on the Drama (c. 1754).

376. A Vindication of Natural Society (1756).

377. A Philosophical Inquiry into the Origin of our Ideas of
the Sublime and Beautiful (1756).

378. An Essay Towards an Abridgement of English History (unfinished, 1757).

379. A Discourse Concerning Taste (1757).

380. Annual Register - at first the whole work, subsequently only the historical article (1758 onwards).

381. The Popery Laws in Ireland (a fragment, 1761).

382. A Short Account of a Late Short Administration (1766).

383. Observations on a Late State of the Nation (1769).

384. Thoughts on the Cause of the Present Discontents (April 1770).

385. A Letter to Sir Charles Bingham (on the Irish Absentee Tax, October 1773).

386. Speech on American Taxation (January 1775).

387. Speech on American Conciliation (May 1775).

388. A Letter to the Marquis of Rockingham (on the proposed secession from Parliament of Members opposed to the American War, January 1777).

389. An Address to the King (1777).

390. An Address to the British Colonists in North America (1777).

391. A Letter to the Sheriffs of Bristol (to justify the conduct of the Party on the Habeas Corpus Bill, April 1777).

392. A Letter to the Hon. C.J. Fox (on the state of the parties, October 1777).

393. Two Letters to a Gentleman at Bristol (on Bills relative to the trade of Ireland, April & May 1778).

394. A Letter to the Right Hon. Edmund Pery, Speaker to the Irish House of Commons (on a Bill for the Relief of the Roman Catholics of Ireland, July 1778).

395. A Letter to Thomas Burgh, Esq. (a defence against attacks on Burke in the Irish Parliament (January 1780).

396. Speech on Economical Reform (March 1780).

397. A Letter to John Merlott, Esq. (on Irish affairs, April 1780).

398. A Letter to the Chairman of the Buckinghamshire Meeting for Procuring Parliamentary Reform (April, 1780).

399. Letters and Reflections on the Execution of the Rioters. (July 1780).

400. Speech at the Guildhall, Bristol, Previous to the Election (September 1780); Speech on Declining the Poll (September 1780).

401. A Letter to a Peer of Ireland (to Viscount Kenmare on the Penal Laws against the Roman Catholics of Ireland, February 1782).

402. Reports from the Select Committee of the House of Commons on India: Ninth Report (June 1783); Eleventh Report (1785).

403. Speech on Fox's East India Bill (January 1784).

404. Representation to His Majesty (June 1784).

405. Speech on the Nabob of Arcot's Debts (August 1785).

406. Speeches on the Impeachment of Warren Hastings (February & April 1788).

407. Speech on the Army Estimates (February 1790).

408. Reflections on the Revolution in France (October 1790).

409. A Letter to the Empress of Russia (1791).

410. A Letter to a Member of the National Assembly (May 1791).

411. An Appeal from the New to the Old Whigs August 1791).

412. Thoughts on French Affairs (December 1791).

413. A Letter to Sir Hercules Langrische (on the Roman Catholics in Ireland, February 1792).

414. The Case of the Suffering Clergy of France (published in Evening Mail September 1792).

415. Observations on the Character of the Minority in the Last Session of Parliament (Letter to the Duke of Portland, August 1793 – published as Fifty-Four Articles of Impeachment against the Right Hon. C.J. Fox, 1797).

416. Remarks on the Policy of the Allies (October 1793).

417. Preface to a Translation of the Address of M. Brissot to his Constituents (1794).

418. Report from the Committee Appointed to Inspect the Lords' Journals (April 1794).

419. Thoughts and Details on Scarcity Presented to W. Pitt (1796)

420. <u>A Letter to a Noble Lord</u> (February 1796).

421. <u>Three Letters on a Regicide Peace</u> (1796); <u>Fourth Letter</u>
     <u>(published posthumously 1797)</u>.

422. <u>Three Memorials on French Affairs</u> (published
     posthumously 1797).

LETTERS

Burke was a voluminous correspondent, but he did not believe
in preserving his personal and official letters, whether
written or received by himself. He was probably dissuaded
from getting rid of most of them by the opposition of his
son, Richard; and as it was, he himself stated that he
'destroyed a cartload of them' after Richard died. He
similarly treated most of the undoubtedly numerous Burke
family letters, except those to and from Richard, which he
thought were of some historic importance. There are known to
remain nowadays two thousand letters from his pen and perhaps
nearly twice as many written to him.

423. T.W. Copeland & M.S. Smith (eds.), <u>Checklist of the</u>
     <u>Correspondence of Edmund Burke</u> (CUP, 1955).

  *   *   *   *   *   *   *   *

424. T.W. Copeland and others (eds), <u>Correspondence of Edmund</u>
     <u>Burke</u> (10 vols., CUP, 1958-1978):
     Vol. I (to 1768), ed. T.W. Copeland (1958).
     Vol. II (1768-1774), ed. L.S. Sutherland (1960),
     Vol. III (1774-1778), ed. G.H. Guttridge (1961).
     Vol. IV (1778-1782), ed. J.A. Woods (1963).
     Vol. V (1782-1789), eds. H. Furber & P.J. Marshall (1965).
     Vol. VI (1789-1791), eds. A. Cobban & R.A. Smith (1967).
     Vol. VII (1792-1794), eds. P.J. Marshall & J. A. Woods
     (1968).
     Vol. VIII (1794-1796), ed. R.B. McDowell (1969).
     Vol. IX (1796-1797), eds. R.B. McDowell & J.A. Woods,
     Vol. X (Index), eds. B. Lowe, P.J. Marshall & J.A Woods.
  This is the essential and most comprehensive collection of
Burke's correspondence.

     Other collections of his letters, which are mainly
reflections upon various limited subjects or friends and
acquaintances, are:

425. <u>Original Letters, Principally from Lord Charlemont,</u>
     <u>Edmund Burke, [and] William Pitt, Earl of Chatham, to</u>
     <u>the Right Hon. Henry Flood</u> (1820).

426. R. Therry, <u>Letter to the Right Honourable George Canning</u>
     (1826).
     A pamphlet on Canning's attitude to the Roman Catholic
claims, which includes some of Burke's correspondence with
his son on this subject.

427. Richard Laurence (ed.), <u>Epistolary Correspondence of the</u>
     <u>Right Honourable Edmund Burke and Dr. French Laurence</u>,
     (London, 1827).
     A collection of letters to the lawyer, Dr. French
Laurence, his friend and literary executor.

428. Charles William, Fifth Earl Fitzwilliam & Sir Richard
     Bourke (eds.), <u>Correspondence of the Right Honourable</u>
     <u>Edmund Burke between 1744 and 1797</u> (4 vols., 1844).
     A large collection of letters, but excluding any that had
appeared elsewhere in print, including his <u>Works</u> (see no.
355).

429. Hugh Owen, <u>Two Centuries of Ceramic Art in Bristol</u>
     (1873)
     Contains the correspondence of Burke with his Bristol
friend, Richard Champion.

430. Countess of Minto, <u>Life and Letters of the First Lord</u>
     <u>Minto, 1731-1806</u> (1874).

431. Hugh Law (ed.), <u>Burke's Speeches and Letters on American</u>
     <u>Affairs</u> (Everynan, 1908).

432. J.P. Gilson (ed.), <u>Correspondence of Edmund Burke and</u>
     <u>William Windham</u> (London, 1910).
     Letters between Burke and his friend and disciple.

433. Harold J. Laski (ed.), <u>Letters of Edmund Burke</u>, (OUP,
     1922).
     A selection dealing mainly with Ireland, America and the
French Revolution.

434. <u>Catalogue of the R.B. Adam Library Relating to Dr.</u>
     <u>Samuel Johnson and his Era</u> (3 vols., London, 1929; 4th.
     vol., Buffalo, New York, 1930).
     Vol. I, the portion separately paged and entitled 'Letters
of Edmund Burke.'

435. Ross J.H. Hoffmann, <u>Edmund Burke, New York Agent, With</u>
     his Letters to the <u>New York Assembly and Intimate</u>
     <u>Correspondence with Charles O'Hara, 1761-1776</u>
     (Philadelphia, 1956).

These works contain some letters by Burke:

436. William Smith, <u>The Rights of Citizens, Being an</u>
     <u>Examination of Mr. Paine's Principles Touching</u>
     <u>Government, By a Barrister</u> (Dublin, 1791).

437. J. Almon, <u>Anecdotes of the Life of William Pitt, Earl of</u>
     <u>Chatham</u> (3 vols., 3rd. ed., London, 1793).

438. Theobald Wolfe Tone, <u>The Autobiography of Theobald</u>
     <u>Wolfe Tone 1763-1798</u>.

439. Theobald Wolfe Tone, <u>The Life of Theobald Wolfe</u>
     <u>Tone Written by Himself and Continued by his Son</u> (2
     vols., Washington, 1826).

440. Percival Stockdale, <u>Memoirs of the Life and Writings of</u>
     <u>Percival Stockdale, Written by Himself</u> (2 vols., London,
     1809).

441. Jesse Foot, <u>The Life of Arthur Murphy</u> (London, 1811).

442. F. Hardy, <u>Memoirs of the Life of the Earl of Charlemont</u>
     (1810).

443. Sir George Thomas Staunton, <u>Memoir of the Life and</u>
     <u>Family of Sir Leonard Staunton</u> (London, 1823).

444. James Prior, <u>Edmund Burke</u> (see no. 160).

445. Frances Dorothy Cartwright, <u>The Life and Correspondence</u>
     <u>of Major Cartwright</u> (2 vols., London, 1826).

446. <u>The Poetical Works of the Revd, George Crabbe, with his</u>
     <u>Letters and Journals, and his Life, by his Son</u> (8 vols.,
     London, 1834)

447. William Roberts, <u>Memoirs of the Life and Correspondence</u>
     <u>of Mrs. Hannah More</u> (4 vols., London, 1834).

448. Charles John Shore, Second Baron Teignmouth, <u>A Memoir</u>
     <u>of the Life and Correspondence of John, Lord</u>
     <u>Teignmouth</u> (2 vols., London, 1843).

449. Mary Leadbeater, <u>Memoirs and Letters of R. and E.</u>
     <u>Shackleton</u> (London, 1849).

450. Mary Leadbeater, <u>Leadbeater Papers</u> (2 vols., London,
     1862).

451. C.R. Leslie & T. Taylor, <u>Life and Times of Sir</u>
     <u>Joshua Reynolds</u> (2 vols., London, 1862).

452. J. Parkes & H. Merivale (eds.), <u>Memoirs of Sir</u>
     <u>Philip Francis</u> (2 vols., London 1867).

453. Hugh Owen, <u>Two Centuries of Ceramic Art in Bristol</u>
     (London, 1873).

454. Emma Elliot, Countess of Minto, <u>Life and Letters of the</u>
     <u>First Lord Minto, 1731-1806</u> (3 vols., London 1874).

455. Rene Huchon (tr. Frederick Clarke), <u>George Crabbe and</u>
     <u>His Times</u> (London, 1907).

456. Helen H. Robbins, <u>Our First Ambassador to China: An</u>
     <u>Account of the Life of George, Earl Macartney</u> (London,
     (London, 1908)

457. Alfred Spencer (ed.), <u>Memoirs of William Hickey</u> (4
     vols., London, 1913-1925).

458. D.D. Wallace, <u>Life of Henry Laurens</u> (London, 1915).

459. Ernest Hartley Coleridge, <u>Life of Thomas Coutts</u> (2 vols., London, 1920).

460. Sophia Weitzman, <u>Warren Hastings and Philip Francis</u> (Manchester, 1929).

461. Frederick W. Hilles, <u>The Literary Life of Sir Joshua Reynolds</u> (CUP, 1936).

462. E. H. Fellowes & E. Pine (eds.), <u>The Tenbury Letters</u> (London, 1942).

463. Philip S. Foner (ed.), <u>The Complete Writings of Thomas Paine</u>, (2 vols., New York, 1945).

464. C. P. Courtney, <u>Montesquieu and Burke</u> (see no. 206).

465. David M. Little & George M. Kahrl (eds.), <u>Letters of David Garrick</u> (3 vols., Cambridge, Mass., 1963).

466. Garland Cannon, <u>The Letters of Sir William Jones</u> (2 vols. OUP, 1970).

POETRY

467. <u>Translation of an Idyllium of Theocritus</u> (1744).

468. <u>Several Scenes of a Play on the Subject of Alfred the Great</u> (1744).

469. <u>Lines on the River Blackwater</u> (1745).

470. <u>Translation of the Concluding Portion of the Second Georgic of Vergil</u> (1746).

471. <u>Lines to John Damer, Esquire</u> (1747).

472. <u>The Reformer</u> (Periodical Paper published in Dublin, 1748).

473. <u>Ballitore, A Short Poem</u> (1754).

Contemporaries of Burke

WILLAM DOWDESWELL (1721-1775)

Educated at Westminster and Christ Church, Oxford, Dowdeswell also studied at Leiden in 1745. He was a Member of Parliament for Tewkesbury from 1747 to 1754 and for Worcester from 1761 to 1775. He was accounted an old-style Tory, but he became friendly with Rockingham, who made him his Chancellor of the Exchequer during the period of his brief ministry from 1765 to 1766. He became with Burke a prominent leader of the Rockingham group in opposition in the House of Commons and supported him during the American crisis.

474. Dorothy Marshall, Eighteenth-Century England (Longmans, 1962).

475. J.B. Owen, The Eighteenth Century, 1714-1815 (Nelson, 1974).

CHARLES JAMES FOX (1749-1806)

A brilliant speaker and accomplished linguist, but also a heavy gambler and drinker, Fox entered Parliament in 1768. He gained attention by his anti-Wikesite speeches and was given junior ministerial posts by Lord North, but broke with him in 1774 and gave Burke valuable support over the American question. He served with Burke in the governments of Rockingham and Portland, being a Secretary of State. They were allies in the India Bill of 1783 and (when they were both again in opposition) the impeachment of Warren Hastings; but Fox's support of the French Revolution dissolved their friendship and left him almost without support in the House of Commons. In its obituary of him, The Times of 15th. September 1806 stated, 'As Mr. Burke has observed, and when he was in intimate friendship with him, his faults, though they might tarnish the lustre and sometimes impede the march of his abilities, were not formed to extinguish the fire of great virtues.'

476. David Schweitzer, Charles James Fox 1749 - 1806: A Bibliography, (Greenwood Press, Westport., Conn. 1992).

477. J.B. Trotter, Memoirs of the Latter Years... of Charles James Fox (1811).

478. Lord John Russell (ed.), Memorials and Correspondence of Charles James Fox (4 vols., 1853-1857).

479. Sir G.O. Trevelyan, The Early History of Charles James Fox (Nelson, 1880).

480. J.L. Hammond, Charles James Fox, A Political Study (Methuen, 1903).

481. Christopher Hobhouse, Fox (John Murray, 1934).

482. E.C.P. Lascelles, The Life of Charles James Fox (OUP, 1936).

483. J.A. Cannon, The Fox-North Coalition (CUP, 1969).

484. L. Reid, Charles James Fox, A Man for the People (Longmans, 1969).

485. L. Mitchell, Charles James Fox and the Disintegration of the Whig Party, 1782-1794 (OUP, 1971).

486. John W. Derry, Charles James Fox (Longmans, 1972).

487. B.W. Hill, 'Fox and Burke: The Whig Party and the Question of Principles,' English Historical Review, vol. vol. LXXXXIX, no. 350 (1974), pp. 1-24.

488. David Powell, Charles James Fox: Man of the People (Hutchinson, 1989).

489. Stanley Ayling, Fox: The Life of Charles James Fox (John Murray, 1991).

PHILIP FRANCIS (1740-1818)

Born in Dublin and educated at St. Paul's School, London, Francis became a clerk in several goverment departments and in 1774 was made one of the four newly-appointed councillors of the Governor-General of India. He violently opposed Warren Hastings and was injured by him in a duel. Leaving India with a large fortune in 1780, he became a Member of Parliament in 1784 and became intimate with Burke in order to continue his campaign against Hastings. He helped Burke prepare the charges against Hastings and assisted the managers of his impeachment. He is commonly supposed to have been the anonymous author of the Letters of Junius (1769-1772) which attacked the administrations of Grafton and Lord North. Dr. Johnson in 1779 believed they could have been written by Burke, who denied this.

490. J. Parkes & H. Merivale (eds.), Memoirs of Philip Francis (2 vols., 1867).

491. Leslie Stephen, 'Chatham, Francis and Junius,' English Historical Review, vol. III (1888), pp. 233-249.

DAVID GARRICK (1717-1779)

For a short time a pupil of Dr. Johnson at Lichfield, Garrick went with him to London. After failing to set up in business, he made his reputation as an actor in 1741 and came to dominate the London stage for nearly thirty years. He frequented the Grecian Coffee House and introduced Burke to Dr. Johnson in 1758. He often entertained Burke and lent him money in 1769 (see nos. 846, 847).

492. Margaret Barton, David Garrick (Faber & Faber, 1948).

KING GEORGE III (1738-1820)

For a century and a half the prevalent view of George III's part in politics during the first years of his reign owed much in origin to Burke's Some Thoughts on the Cause of the Present Discontents (1770). He considered that the King was intent upon restoring the absolute authority enjoyed by the Stuart monarchs in the previous century. Since, however, Sir Lewis Namier's research (see nos. 537, 538), it has been impossible to believe this. In fact, the Revolutionary Settlement of 1688 had left the Crown considerable powers, and was justified in his wish to choose his own ministers, but his political inexperience made the first ten years of his reign a period of political uncertainty. This publication of Burke was a piece of political propaganda designed to support the Rockingham Whigs as opposed to the 'King's Friends.' Also, since George was then young, unmarried and likely to reign for a long time, opposition politicians could not justify their resistance to the Crown by claiming to support the interests of his heir, so Burke set out a new idea for this, which became the basis of modern party politics 'a combination of expedients was changed into a system of general principles' [Lord Acton, Lectures on Modern History (Collins, 1960), p. 261.]

493. Richard Pares, King George III and the Politicians (OUP, 1954).

494. R.J. White, The Age of George III (Heinemann, 1968).

495. J. Brooke, King George III (Constable, 1972).

GEORGE GRENVILLE (1712-1770)

The younger brother of Lord Temple and brother-in-law of the Elder Pitt, Grenville was a member of the famous Grenville-Lyttleton-Pitt cousinhood which helped to overthrow Sir Robert Walpole in 1742. He held various government posts from 1744 until presiding over his own administration between 1763 and 1765, during which the Stamp Act was passed and the early proceedings begun against John Wilkes. He was an effective, determined administrator and able to master details, but he was unimaginative, short-sighted and lacking in political skill. Burke thought his character was influenced by his training as a barrister (see no. 798).

496. P. Lawson, George Grenville: A Political Life (OUP, 1984).

497. Rory T. Cornish, George Grenville 1712 - 1770: A Bibliography (Greenwood Press, Westport, Conn., 1992).

SAMUEL JOHNSON (1709-1784)

The son of a Lichfield bookseller, Samuel Johnson went to Oxford, but was forced to leave by poverty. He maintained himself as a schoolmaster and a bookseller until he decided to try his fortune in London, where for some years he reported parliamentary debates and wrote articles for magazines. In 1747 he began his Dictionary of the English Language, the first of his important pioneer systematic literary studies.

Largely through James Boswell's biography, he became better known, however, for his personality and opinions, wit and conversation which won him many friends. Burke met him in 1758 and was an original member of the Literary Club, which Johnson founded in 1763 (see no. 610). Burke became one of the most intimate of his friends, and in strength of mind he seems to have been his   only rival at their meetings. Johnson admired him as an orator and valued him as a worthy disputant.

498. John Bailey, Dr.Johnson and His Circle (OUP, 2nd. ed., 1944).

499. Robert Lynd, Dr. Johnson and Company (Penguin Books, 1946).

FREDERICK, LORD NORTH (1732-1792)

A favourite of George III and a man of considerable political experience through service in previous governments, Lord North formed his administration in 1770. Having experienced six administrations during the first ten years of his reign, the King appointed him as a minister upon whom he could rely and could manage the House of Commons. North gave the country six years of settled government, but he had to face the declamations of Burke and Chatham and intractable problem of the revolting American colonies. The King supported him in office, but eventually he had to resign in 1782. His, as Burke recognized, was the misfortune of one who would have been a competent minister in more favourable times (see nos. 956-958).

500. W.B. Pemberton, Lord North (Longmans, Green, 1938).

501. Herbert Butterfield, George III, Lord North and the People 1779-1780 (Bell, 1949).

502. I.R. Christie, The End of North's Ministry 1780-1782 (Macmillan, 1958).

503. A. Valentine, Lord North (University of Oklahoma Press, 2 vols., 1967).

504. P.D.G. Thomas, <u>Lord North</u> (Allen Lane, 1976).

THOMAS PAINE (1737-1809)

The acknowledged leader and spokesman of the extreme redicalism of his time, Paine was the son of a small Norfolk farmer. He became an excise officer in 1761, but was dismissed from the service for agitating for the removal of grievances. In 1774 he went to America with a note of introduction from Benjamin Franklin, and two years later achieved fame with the publication of his <u>Common Sense</u> in which he urged the revolting colonies to declare their immediate independence from British rule. Returning to England, he published in 1791, in reply to Burke's <u>Reflections on the Revolution in France</u>, the first part of his <u>Rights of Man</u>, which was a defence of the principles of the Revolution against Burke's aspersions and a statement of the ultimate political rights of the British people. A year later, when he issued the second part, advocating positive projects of social reform, he had to flee to France to escape prosecution for treason, the book having rapidly become a manifesto of those who sympathised with the Revolution. He was at once elected a member of the Convention and made a citizen of the new revolutionary state, but in 1793, on account of his opposition to the execution of Louis XVI, he was imprisoned until the death of Robespierre. He published his deistic tract, <u>The Age of Reason</u>, in 1794 and from 1802 spent the last years of his life in America in ostracism and poverty.

505. Hesketh Pearson, <u>Tom Paine, Friend of Mankind</u> (Hamish Hamilton, 1937).

506. H.N. Brailsford, <u>Shelley, Godwin and their Circle</u> (OUP, 1945).

507. R.R. Fennessy, <u>Burke, Paine and the Rights of Man: A Difference of Political Opinion</u> (Martinus Nijhoff, The Hague, 1963).

508. Francis P. Canavan, ' The Burke-Paine Controversy,' <u>Political Science Reviewer</u>, vol. VI (1976), pp. 389-420.

509. A. Owen Aldridge, <u>Thomas Paine's American Ideology</u> (University of Delaware Press, 1984).

510. David Powell, <u>Tom Paine: The Greatest Exile</u> (Hutchinson, 1987).

511. A.J. Ayer, <u>Thomas Paine</u> (Martin Secker & Warburg, 1988).

WILLIAM PITT, FIRST EARL OF CHATHAM (1708-1778)

By the time Burke entered Parliament in 1765, Pitt's great days were over. For five years from 1756 he had directed the Seven Years' War against France, obtaining such achievement as Clive's victories in India and Wolfe's capture of Quebec. He was the 'pilot who weathered the storm' until 1761, when

he resigned because he would not accept the desire of the
King and the administration to bring hostilities to an end.
The fall of the Rockingham ministry in 1766, three years
after the conclusion of the War, brought him back into
office, but by then he was a changed man. The 'great
Commoner' had gone into the House of Lords as Earl of
Chatham, and he was subject to increasingly severe bouts of
mental instability. He failed to unite his ministry and
resigned in 1768, to spend the rest of his time in opposition
until he collapsed in 1778 after speaking in favour of the
withdrawal of British forces from America.

Burke could probably have had a place in his short-lived
government, but he disliked him for his opposition to
Rockingham and considered him dictatorial in his manner (see
nos. 823-824). He now spoke of him always with criticism and
resentment; but the epitaph on the memorial to Pitt in the
Guildhall, which he composed for the citizens of London,
states that it was inscribed, 'That they may never meet for
the transaction of their affairs without being reninded that
the means by which Providence raises a nation to greatness
are the virtues infused into a great man.'

512. A.F.B. Williams, The Life of William Pitt, Earl of
     Chatham (2 vols., Longmans, 1913).

513. Brian Tunstall, William Pitt, Earl of Chatham (Hodder &
     Staughton, 1938).

514. John Brooke, The Chatham Administration, 1766-1768
     (Macmillan, 1956).

515. S. Ayling, The Elder Pitt, Earl of Chatham (John Murray,
     1976).

516. Jeremy Black, Pitt the Elder (CUP, 1993).

WILLIAM PITT THE YOUNGER (1759-1806)

The second son of the Earl of Chatham, Pitt entered the House
of Commons in 1780 and attached himself to the Shelburne
Whigs in opposition to North's ministry. His maiden speech
was in support of Burke's economical reform, who expressed
his admiration of him (see no. 945). After being Chancellor
of the Exchequer in Shelburne's short-lived administration,
he came to power in 1783 and held his post with a brief
interlude for the remaining twenty-three years of his life,
during which time he restored the national finances after the
American rebellion, settled the administration of India and
led the country in the war against France.

He was convinced by Burke's charges against Hastings, and
by his support made the impeachment possible, but he opposed
Burke over the Regency question. When he broke with Fox in
1791, Burke crossed the floor of the House and sat next to
Pitt on the Treasury Bench. On the outbreak of war, Burke
wished Pitt to recognize that it would be a long war, urged
him to support the French Royalists and opposed attempts to
enter into negotiations for peace (see nos. 1122, 1138).

517. J.W. Derry, William Pitt (Batsford, 1962).

518. J. Ehrman, <u>The Younger Pitt</u> (Constable, 2 vols., 1969-1983).

519. Derek Jarrett, <u>Pitt the Younger</u> (Weidenfeld & Nicolson, 1974).

520. A.D. Harvey, <u>William Pitt the Younger 1759-1806: A Bibliography</u> (Greenwood Press, Westport, Conn., 1989).

RICHARD PRICE (1723-1791)

Educated at a Dissenting Academy in London, Richard Price officiated at several Unitarian congregations. He established a reputation through his <u>Review of the Principal Questions in Morals</u> and in the same year was made a Doctor of Divinity by Glasgow University. Subsequently he became known as a writer on financial questions. He opposed the action against the American colonies, and after the war, being consulted by Pitt about the best way of liquidating the national debt, is said to have persauded him to adopt the sinking fund.

His fame in after years has rested upon the sermon which he preached at the Meeting House in Old Jewry before the Revolution Society in 1789 on Psalm 122 and published as <u>A Discourse on the Love of Our Country</u>. Burke had already disagreed over the American question with Price, who had supported the colonists on claims of natural rights and abstract principles of justice, while he did so on grounds of expediency; and in his <u>Reflections on the Revolution in France</u>, he held this was a disaster brought about by such ideas. Price died before the outbreak of the Terror in France which strengthed Burke's case.

521. D.O. Thomas, <u>The Honest Mind; The Thought and Work of Richard Price</u> (OUP, 1977).

CHARLES, SECOND MARQUIS OF ROCKINGHAM(1730-1782)

A wealthy landowner in Yorkshire and a member of the old Whig aristocracy, Rockingham entered politics because he felt that his position required that he should do so and rarely spoke in the House of Lords. When Grenville had lost George III's confidence an the support of the trading classes, he was persuaded in 1765 to form a government and appointed Burke as his private secretary, who exercised a powerful influence upon him (see no. 812). Rockingham inherited the dangerously difficult situation caused by American resistance to the Stamp Act and was able to repeal it in 1766, but had to conciliate the opposition by simultaneously passing the Declaratory Act. Disunity in his Cabinet and lack of the King's confidence undermined his power, and he lost office in 1766.

In opposition Rockingham and his followers formed one of the groups of Whigs seeking office. Burke was their chief spokesman in the House of Commons, and the publication in 1770 of his <u>Some Thoughts on the Cause of the Present Discontents</u> revolutionized their position and, indeed, the whole idea of the party system. Rockingham and Burke also acted together in advocating Economical Reform and independence for America, and when Lord North's fall from

office in 1782 brought about Rockingham's second ministry,
the King had to agree to both of these. Burke made a
contribution towards the first, but the second had not been
achieved when the ministry was brought to an end by
Rockingham's sudden death. He was commonly regarded as an
ineffectual leader, but Burke believed him to be a man of
'honour and integrity' and able to establish good human
relationships (see no. 811).

522. George Thomas Keppel, Earl of Albemarle, Memoirs of the
     Marquis of Rockingham and His Contemporaries (2 vols.,
     1852).

523. P. Langford, The First Rockingham Ministry, 1765-1766
     (OUP, 1973).

524. R.J.S. Hoffman, The Marquis: A Study of Lord Rockingham
     1730-1782 (Fordham University Press, New York, 1973).

525. J. Brewer. 'Rockingham, Burke and Whig Political
     Argument,' Historical Journal, vol. XVIII (1975), pp.
     118-201.

526. Frank O'Gorman, The Rise of Party in England: The
     Rockingham Whigs, 1789-1782 (Allen & Unwin, 1975).

WILLIAM, SECOND EARL OF SHELBURNE (1737-1805)

When Lord North finally resigned in 1782, Lord Shelburne
became Home Secretary in Rockingham's ministry. He was
described by Disraeli as the 'ablest and most accomplished
minister of the eighteenth century.' He supported
conciliation of the American colonists, freedom of trade,
Roman Catholic emancipation and parliamentary reform, but he
was handicapped throughout his career by his contempt for
political parties and the general mistrust he aroused through
suspicions of insincerity. He had already twice been forced
to resign from government posts through quarrels with his
colleagues - in 1763 after a few months under Grenville and
in 1768 after two years in the Elder Pitt's administration.
Burke called him 'a Borgia and a Cataline, and he considered
Burke's economical reform was 'both framed and carried
through without the least regard to facts.' On Rockingham's
death, he became First Lord of the Treasury, but soon
resigned after a quarrel with Fox and did not hold office
again.

527. Edmund George Petty, Baron Fitzmaurice, William, Earl
     of Shelburne (2nd.& rev. ed., 1912, 2 vols., Macmillan,
     1912).

RICHARD BRINSLEY SHERIDAN (1751-1816)

Noted as a dramatist and Parliamentary orator, Sheridan was,
like Burke, born in Ireland. His brilliant wit made him a
public figure and marked the three great comedies, which he
wrote during his brief but brilliant five years as a
dramatist - The Rivals, The School for Scandal and The
Critic. Through Dr. Johnson and membership of the Literary

Club, he became a very close friend of Burke and Fox. From writing political essays, he went on to enter Parliament in 1780 as a supporter of Fox and held a number of important appointments. From then on his career was mainly that of an orator and politician. Though not sharing Burke's views on India, he made two famous speeches during the impeachment of Warren Hastings. He strenuously opposed British policy in America, but approved the French Revolution, which led Burke to break with him in 1791. He ended his life increasingly drunken, unfaithful to his wife and disappointed and dissolute.

528. R.C. Rhodes, The Plays and Poems of Richard Brinsley Sheridan with a Bibliography (OUP, 1928).

529. Stanley Ayling, A Portrait of Sheridan (John Murray, 1985.

CHARLES TOWNSHEND (1725-1767)

Described by Burke as 'the most brilliant man of his or any age' and 'the delight and ornament of the House of Commons,' but nicknamed the 'Weathercock' because of his alleged instability and lack of principle, Townshend became Chancellor of the Exchequer in 1766 in the ministry of Chatham, whose illness enabled him to defy his colleagues and induce Parliament to accept in 1767 his ill-fated taxes upon tea and other goods imported by the American colonies. Burke's verdict on him was, 'To please universally was the object of his life; but to tax and to please, no more than to love and be wise, is not given to man.' However, he possessed charm and ability, and some of the best judges placed his eloquence above that of Burke, and but for his early death he might have led an adminitration. [RM, p. 159; AS, pp. 72-73]

530. P.H. Fitzgerald, Charles Townshend (1866).

JOHN WILKES (1725-1797)

The son of a well-to-distiller, Wilkes was educated at a private school at Hertford and at the University of Leyden. His father married him to an elderly heiress, whom he deserted after using her fortune to advance his career. He became High Sheriff of Buckinghamshire in 1754 and Member of Parliament for Aylesbury in 1757. He sought prestige and popularity by attacking George III's administration, especially in the weekly newspaper, The North Briton, founded by him. After describing the King's speech as false in no. 45 in 1763, he was expelled from the House of Commons and went abroad for four years. On his return, he was thrice elected for Middlesex with large majorities, but was not allowed to sit in Parliament until 1774; he remained a member until 1790. Though a debauchee and a political adventurer, he had great constitutional importance in upholding individual and parliamentary rights. His 'cause' but not 'the person' won the support of Burke, who presented a petition against his expulsion from the House, and they both opposed the government during the contest with America.

531. William Purdie Treloar, Wilkes and the City (John Murray, 1917).

532. O.A. Sherrard, A Life of John Wilkes (Allen & Unwin, 1930).

533. George Rude, Wilkes and Liberty (OUP, 1962).

534. C.C. Trench, Portrait of a Patriot, A Biography of John Wilkes (Blackwood, Edinburgh), 1962).

CHRISTOPHER WYVILL (1740-1822)

The Revd. Christopher Wyvill was educated at Queens' College, Cambridge, and became Rector of a parish in Essex. In 1779 he became Secretary of the Yorkshire Association, which had been formed to secure efficient and incorrupt government, shorter parliaments and equalization of representation; and the next year he persuaded it to present the Yorkshire petition to the House of Commons. This resembled the earlier Wilkesite campaign, but attracted more influential and propertied men. The opposition to Lord North accepted the movement's support, but did not entirely accept its aims, and later Burke's economical reforms satisfied most of its members. In later life, Wyvill published many works advocating religious toleration and parliamentary reform.

535. I.R. Christie, Wilkes, Wyvill and Reform, (Macmillan, 1962).

The Political Background

In the Britain of the eighteenth century, every Member of the House of Commons represented either a county or a borough. Most of the counties and boroughs each returned two Members, but the right to vote was not the same in the two sorts of constituencies.

In all the counties it had been the same since it was fixed by Act of Parliament 1430. It was possessed by men who owned freehold property valued at forty shillings (£2) a year. Since the value of money had declined considerably during the intervening centuries, the number of county voters had steadily increased. It has been reckoned that all the English counties had an average of about four thousand electors each, ranging from about sixteen thousand in Yorkshire, the largest, to about six hundred in Rutland, the smallest. It is impossible to arrive at accurate figures because county elections were very expensive and uncertain, so they were rarely contested.

In the boroughs there was a great variety of franchises, largely depending upon local medieval customs. In a few almost all men had the vote, but in most it was limited to classes such as ratepayers, householders, burgesses (or freemen), members of the corporation or burgage-holders (who were owners of certain properties). This usually meant that the electorate in each was small. Less than a tenth of the English boroughs had more than a thousand voters. Moreover, owing to a dispute between Crown and Parliament in the later seventeenth century as to which had the right to create new constituencies, the number of boroughs had remained unaltered since then. Many boroughs were very small places, and some were 'rotten boroughs,' which had become seriously depopulated over the years. The smallness of the boroughs, their restricted electorate and the system of open voting also led to 'pocket boroughs' in which the representation was controlled by big landowners.

The working of the contemporary franchise is illustrated by Burke's political career. In 1765 Lord Verney, through his extensive land-owning in Buckinghamshire, enabled Burke to present himself for election by Wendover, a small market-town which was a pocket borough in which 160 householders had the vote, and he was returned without difficulty. The influence

of such a patron was was a way which made possible a
political career for able men without the advantages of
birth, money or influence. Neither Burke nor Sheridan would
have been able to enter Parliament otherwise.

Though Burke was an established politician when he stood
as a candidate for Bristol in 1774, the second largest city
in Britain, he was now in a different political position.
Here the vote was possessed by the forty-shilling freeholders
(as in the counties) and the free burgesses, numbering five
thousand in all, who were mostly merchants and commonly
returned men of their own class to Parliament. He had,
therefore, for the first time genuinely to contest an
election. Moreover, while he had represented his previous
constituency, since he and Lord Verney had shared the same
political outlook, he had enjoyed considerable freedom in
word and deed; but the electors of Bristol expected their
Members of Parliament to promote their specific interests.
Despite his claim to them that he possessed the right to be
independence, experience compelled him to learn that he could
not exercise this when representing Bristol (see nos. 934-
938.

Their assertiveness led him to decline the poll in 1780 at
the city, but he was needed in Parliament by Rockingham, who
arranged for him to be returned for one of his pocket
boroughs, Malton in Yorkshire. There the three hundred
burgage-holders used their vote as as required and never
sought to put pressure upon their representative.

Throughout his political career, Burke opposed attempts
made by Pitt and others to implement measures of
parliamentary reform (see nos. 849-851; 916-918); but during
period of some thirty years when he was in the House of
Commons, though never holding an important government post,
he was involved in two British constitutional developments.
These were his contribution to the political structure of the
eighteenth century and his general political philosophy. The
first was most forcibly stated in his Thoughts on the
Cause of the Present Discontents (1770) and the second in his
Reflections on the Revolution in France (1790).

The Thoughts was his answer to the crisis aroused by
Wilkes and the Middlesex election. He asserted that this
conflict between Parliament had been caused by George III's
alleged undue intervention in the government of the
country,which had been made possible by the current political
situation. Since 1714 the Whigs had been predominant in
Parliament, but they did not act as a united party. Rather
they were split into personalized groups, each of about ten
members. The Rockingham Whigs were exceptional in having some
eighty members. Burke insisted that they alone could provide
firm, independent government that should not be motivated
merely by personal interests and connections, but must be 'a
body of men united for promoting by their joint efforts the
national interest upon some principle in which they are all
agreed.' He wished them to act consistently upon this basis
in opposition and enter office upon their own terms, which
they finally did in 1782. This was to establish the party-
system in place of the factional contests which had
dominated politics.

The French Revolution brought about a revival of the
political strength of the Tories, and Burke's Reflections

provided them with their philosophy. The Foxites, who supported the revolutionaries and parliamentary reform, styled themselves as Whigs and designated their opponents as Tories, who came to accept the term. Among the ideas in the Reflections which they accepted were social continuity, gradual change instead of violent revolution - 'Make the Revolution a parent of settlement and not a nursery of future revolutions;' the value of an aristocracy - 'Nobility is a graceful order to the civil society. It is the Corinthian capital of polished society;' the inevitability of inequality - 'A perfect democracy is therefore the most shameless thing in the world.'

536. Edward Porrit, The Unreformed House of Commons, 2 vols., (CUP, 1903; repr. New York, 1963).

537. Sir Lewis Namier, The Structure of Politics at the Accession of George III (Macmillan, 1928; 2nd. ed., 1961).

538. Sir Lewis Namier, England in the Age of the American Revolution (Macmillan, 1930; 2nd. ed., 1957).

539. A.S. Foord, 'The Waning of the Influence of the Crown,' English Historical Review, vol. LXII (1947).

540. W.J. Christie, Myth and Reality in Late Eighteenth-Century Politics (Macmillan, 1970).

541. P.D.G.Thomas, The House of Commons in the Eighteenth Century (OUP, 1971).

542. F. O'Gorman, The Rise of Party in England: the Rockingham Whigs (Allen & Unwin, 1975).

543. F. O'Gorman, The Emergence of the British Two-Party System (Arnold, 1982).

544. B. W. Hill, British Parliamentary Parties, 1742-1832 (Allen & Unwin, 1985).

545. F. O'Gorman, 'The Unreformed Electorate of Hanoverian England: The Mid-Eighteenth Century to the Reform Act of 1832,' Social History, vol. XI (1986), pp. 33-52.

546. P.D.T., Thomas, 'Party Politics in Eighteenth-Century Britain: Some Myths and a Touch of Reality,' British Journal of Eighteenth-Century Studies, vol. X (1987).

547. J.R. Dinwiddy, Radicalism and Reform in Britain, 1780-1850 (Hambledon Press, 1992).

ADMINISTRATIVE AND FINANCIAL REFORM

Although Burke refused to give his support to any of the eighteenth-century attempts at parliamentary reform, which were mainly concerned with the enlargement of the franchise and the more equitable distribution of seats, he took the lead in initiating administrative and financial reforms that would free Parliament from royal interference. The widespread public resentment at the mounting expense of the American War during the last years of Lord North's administration gave him the opportunity to do this. By representing his policy of 'economical reform' as an attack on corruption and administrative inefficiency, he planned to transfer the patronage administered by the King and North to the parliamentary opposition without making concessions to the cause of parliamentary reform.

In February 1780 he introduced into the House of Commons his bill 'for the Better Security of the Independence of Parliament and the Economical Reformation of the Civil and other Establishments.' This proposed an extensive reduction in the royal household, the suppression of many offices of state, including the entire abolition of the Board of Trade, the sale of most of the Crown lands and a reform of the pension list and various government departments.

The idea of economy gained much support in the Commons, but members feared Burke's measure would upset the balance of the constitution. North was able to secure the defeat of all his proposals except the abolition of the Board of Trade. He remained in office for another two troubled years.

When the Rockingham Whigs gained power in 1782, Burke was determined to use his position as Paymaster General to make another effort to put his ideas of economical reform into practice. This time he was more successful. His Civil List Act (or Establishment Act) was passed in 1782. It was not as extensive as his previous proposals owing to the continued hostility towards such measures, but it did forbid government contractors to sit in Parliament, disfranchised some thousands of revenue officers and excise men, abolished more than forty valuable offices in the King's gift and reduced the pension list and secret service money.

The purpose of Burke and his supporters was still not to abolish the system of patronage. They considered this to be politically necessary, but wanted to prevent it from acting as a means of royal influence, which they believed could be used particularly against politicians who opposed the Crown. Burke, indeed, did not hesitate, at the same time as he was seeking to put his ideas of economical reform into practice, to obtain sinecures for his friends and relations (see nos. 986-987).

548. E. Hughes, Studies in Administration and Finance, 1558-1825 (Manchester UP, 1934).

549. J.E.D. Binney, British Public Finance and Administration 1774-1792 (OUP, 1958).

550. H. Rosaveare, The Treasury, 1660-1870: The Foundations of Control (Allen & Unwin, 1973).

POLITICIANS AND THE AMERICAN COLONIES

The Treaty of Paris of 1763, which brought to an end the Seven Years' War, changed the position of the thirteen British colonies in North America. It gave Britain possession Canada and the other French settlements there. The colonists

were freed from the threat both to their existence and to
their prospects of further expansion. The British government
had never been able to exercise strict control over them.
They had been able to develop their own way of life and
institutions, and now a new sense of freedom and opportunity
appeared among the politically conscious of the colonists.

This was expressed most strongly by the American
politicians, who were mainly a group of educated men, writers
and thinkers, such as Samuel Adams, Benjamin Franklin, James
Otis and Thomas Jefferson; they were supported by a set of
radicals of little education or none, mainly backwoodsmen and
mechanics, who were to give the revolutionary movement, once
it started, much of its violent energy. These two groups
remained a small minority among the colonists, even when
fighting actually began, but they were the most politically
active and conscious, and so determined to used American
grievances (caused by Parliament's measures from 1765
onwards) to resist the British government that no concessions
it might have made would have placated them for long.

At the same time, the end of hostilities brought Britain
fresh problems. The War had been expensive, and continuing
expenditure was required by the greatly-enlarged overseas
possessions. The landlords and merchants in Parliament
particularly wanted taxation to be reduced by placing a
larger share of the cost of imperial administration and
defence upon the colonies, which were widely believed not to
have imposed adequate taxes to meet the government's wartime
needs. And an uprising of the Indians of the Ohio valley in
1763 convinced the government that a permanent military force
was needed in America.

American protest at the several financial measures imposed
on the colonies flared into open rebellion when penalties had
been imposed upon the colony of Massachusetts after the
demonstration of resistance known as the Boston Tea Party of
1773. Armed resistance began in 1775 with the engagement at
Lexington.

Among the British politicians, Townshend and Lord North
have been blamed particularly for the outbreak of the War of
Independence, but parliamentary and public opinion agreed
with their measures. There was a general feeling that the
extreme minority in the colonies took advantage of every
concession made by Britain and must sooner or later be
confronted by an assertion of its imperial sovereignty.
George III too has been accused of personal responsibility
for the loss of the colonies, but in so far as this was so it
was because her persistently and obstinately supported the
efforts of his ministers to assert parliamentary sovereignty
over the colonies.

Chatham, Burke and Fox were the three leading British
politicians to oppose them. Burke condemned the
administration for governing its relations with the American
colonies by legalistic procedure. He wanted to undo all the
mischief occasioned by the legalistic dispute over taxation
and parliamentary rights and establish a relationship of
unsuspecting confidence between the mother country and the
colonies.He typically based his arguments on expediency and
not principle. But two are needed for conciliation. He did
not realize that such a solution was now impossible. The

repeal of the controversial legislation would not have bound
the colonies closer to Britain, but rather have enabled them
to gain that virtual independence which they now desired.
British public opinion would not have been satisfied with a
mere nominal sovereignty over the colonies, nor would Burke,
who believed that Britain could retain commercial control
over them.

As Lord Brougham, himself a Radical and a politician with
long parliamentary experience, later realized (see no. 1148),
had either Burke or Fox been in power that would sooner or
later have found that conciliation was unacceptable in
America and surrender unthinkable in Britain. Concessions
with regard to taxation and legislation to the colonies would
not affect the explicit acknowledgement of Parliament's
supremacy which both men required from the American leaders.
They too would have been compelled to embark upon war.

551. W.T. Laprade, 'The Stamp Act in British Politics,'
American Historical Review, vol. XXXV (1932), p. 375.

552. G.H. Guttridge, English Whiggism and the American
Revolution (University of California Press, Berkeley &
Los Angeles, 1942).

553. C.R. Ritcheson, The Ideological Origins of the American
Revolution (University of Oklahoma Press, 1954).

554. B. Bailyn, The Ideological Origins of the American
Revolution (Cambridge, Mass., 1967).

555. A.G. Olson, Anglo-American Politics, 1660-1775: The
Relationship between Parties in England and Colonial
America (OUP, 1973).

556. P.D.G. Thomas, British Politics and the Stamp Act Crisis
1763-1767 (OUP, 1975).

557. L. Heren, The Story of America (Times Books, 1976).

THE EAST INDIA COMPANY

Once the Spanish Armada had been defeated in 1588, England
could embark upon overseas commercial ventures. Much of this
was undertaken by the newly-established joint-stock
companies. These included the Muscovy Company, the Royal
African Company, the Virginia Company and the Massachusetts
Bay Company, but the greatest was the East India Company.
This was founded by charter of Queen Elizabeth I in 1600 as
'The Governor and Company of Merchants of London trading into
the East Indies.' Its original purpose was to intrude upon
Portugal's trade with the Spice Islands of the Malay
Archipelago, but the Dutch were already doing this, and when,
by the Amboyna Massacre of 1623, they destroyed one of the
small scattered English trading-posts, the Company had to
move to the Indian mainland.

The first trading-post or 'factory' established there by
the Company was at Surat in 1608, but by the early eighteenth
century the three most important, called presidencies, were
at Madras, Bombay and Calcutta. The Company raised troops and

a fleet of East Indiamen, merchant ships that brought to
England cargoes of silk and calico, tea and coffee, spices
and drugs. From 1708 administrative control of the Company
was in the hands of the Court of twenty-four Directors (six
of whom retired in turn each year), chosen by the larger
shareholders.

The eighteenth-century rivalry and hostilities between
Britain and France spread to India, and the competing French
company sought to take advantage of the decline of the Mogul
Empire to gain control of an increasing area in India. The
victories of Robert Clive (1725-1774), culminating in the
Battle of Plassey in 1757, established the supremacy of the
Company. This also brought about a revolutionary change in
its position and functions. Hitherto it had been a trading
corporation   with   no   territorial   or   administrative
responsibilities. It now became a governing authority as
well. All Bengal, with a population twice that of England and
immense land revenues, came under its control, and it entered
upon an irreversible process of further conquest and rule.

Having been formed for trade, however, the Company was not
well-suited to exercise political power. Its officials were
inexperienced or unscrupulous. Clive suggested to Pitt in
1759 that the Crown should take over from the Company the
management of the newly-conquered territories, but Pitt was
too preoccupied with the conduct of the Seven Years' War to
consider this question. Clive stated, before his departure to
England in 1764, that the great threat to Bengal was now that
of 'venality and corruption.'

When he returned to India as Governor of Bengal from 1765
to 1767, he succeeded during that short time in implementing
reforms, which effected a temporary improvement in the
situation, but when he returned to England he faced hatred
from the 'nabobs,' the wealthy, retired Company officials. In
1772 his enemies secured the appointment of a parliamentary
commission to examine his whole conduct in India, including
his financial transactions - about which he said, 'I stand
astonished at my own moderation!' The commission acknowledged
that he had 'rendered great and meritorious services to his
country,' but would not fully exonerate him, and in 1774
depression and sickness drove him to suicide.

Clive was followed in India by officials of no great
ability, and many of the old abuses reappeared, while the
great famine of 1770 seriously reduced the Company's revenue.
It was clear that the Company was incapable of ruling
millions of people and was also in serious financial
difficulties. From 1767 to 1771 corruption and famine
together caused the Company's revenue to fall by £400,000 a
year, while its military expenses rose by £160,000 in the
same period. Economy was impossible as the shareholders
pressed for higher dividends. The Company moved further and
further towards bankruptcy; it was compelled to borrow until
it faced financial disaster and the possibility of losing its
tradng charter.

It sought to save the situation appointing Warren Hastings
(1732-1818) to be Governor of Bengal in 1771. He had been in
the service of the Company since the age of seventeen, and
was one of the greatest Englishmen to go to India. The
Directors, keenly aware of 'the general corruption and

rapacity' among their officials, expressed their confidence in his 'great ability and unblemished character.' Finding conditions 'as wild as chaos itself,' Hastings removed the collection of taxes from native administrators and set up a board of revenue, abolished internal trade by the Company's servants and devised a legal system based upon Hindu law.

The Company's financial situation, however, remained desperate. In 1772, after being refused a loan by the Bank of England, the Directors approached the government. Observing the contrast between the Company's plight and the wealth of the nabobs, Lord North's answer was the Regulating Act of 1773, which divided authority in India between the Company and the Crown by vesting the power of administration in a Governor-General, who was to be appointed by the Company, but advised and controlled by a Council of four members appointed by the government.

Hastings was made the first Governor-General. He implemented further reforms, enforced the rules against the acceptance of presents by officials and sought to separate the functions of government from the management of trade, but he faced widespread difficulties. The Directors in London hampered his work and demanded high dividends. He had to defeat armed intervention in India by France after her declaration of war on Britain during the American War of Independence. Above all, the new administrative system at first almost nullified his efforts. Suspicious of the honesty of the Company's officials and sharing the popular dislike of the nabobs, the government appointed to the Council members likely to be critical of the Governor-General. The result was continual friction between him and the Council led by Sir Philip Francis. Only after the Bengal climate had killed two of the councillors and Francis had returned to England in 1780,after being shot by Hastings in a duel, did he have a Council favourable to him.

Meanwhile, the unsatisfactory conditions in India had aroused the concern of Burke, who held that wise and just British rule there must compensate for the mistakes made in America.He probably drafted the India Bill introduced in December 1783, which attempted a simple and drastic solution. It intended that the entire management of the Company's territory and all the appointments that went with it should be handed over to seven commissioners, appointed in the first instance by the government for four years and subsequently by the shareholders. These suggestions alienated the City of London and the nabobs, but popular indignation came with the naming of the proposed new commissioners, who were four Foxites and three supporters of North, including his own son. It seemed that during the four years at their disposal they would be able to secure such a monopoly of Indian patronage for the Foxites that the shareholders would not be able to oppose them. This outcry provoked George III to bring down the government he disliked.

The next year Pitt put his India Act into effect.This set up a Board of Control in India (consisting of a Secretary of State, the Chancellor of the Exchequer and four Privy Councillors)to take charge of all the country's civil, military and judicial affairs. The Governor-General was to be appointed by the Cabinet and assisted by a Council of three members. The Company retained control of its commercial interests and Indian patronage. Hastings, however, disliked its terms. 'It has destroyed all my hopes, both here and at home,' he wrote and immediately resigned.

He returned to England in 1785 to face his enemies. Francis persuaded Burke that Hastings was responsible for the alleged failure of British rule in India. He secured his impeachment in 1788 for corruption and cruelty. The trial lasted seven years during which Burke made some of his most eloquent (and vituperative) speeches for the prosecution, but failed in his case. Public opinion favoured Hastings when he was eventually freed. He was ruined by the proceedings, but the Company pensioned him well - to Burke's indignation.

558. Vincent A. Smith, The Oxford History of India (OUP, 1941).

559. Lucy. S. Sutherland, The East India Company in Eighteenth-Century Politics (OUP, 1952).

560. P.J. Marshall, Problems of Empire: Britain and India. 1757-1813 (Allen & Unwin, 1968).

561. Anonymous, A History of the Trial of Warren Hastings, Esq (Debrett, 1796).

562. G.R. Gleig, Life of Warren Hastings (3 vols., Bentley, 1841).

563. Sydney C. Grier, The Letters of Warren Hastings to his Wife (Blackwood, 1905).

564. Lionel J. Trotter, Life of Warren Hastings (Everyman, 1910).

565. M.E. Monckton-Jones, Warren Hastings in Bengal (OUP, 1918).

566. E.P. Moon, Warren Hastings and British India (Hodder & Stoughton, 1947).

567. Keith Feiling, Warren Hastings (Macmillan, 1954).

568. P.J. Marshall, The Impeachment of Warren Hastings (OUP, 1965).

569. Michael Edwardes, The Nabobs at Home (Constable, 1991).

BRITAIN AND THE FRENCH REVOLUTION

When the French Revolution began in the summer of 1789. British political opinion was largely occupied with the year-old trial of Warren Hastings. Since France was Britain's age-long enemy, such attention as the event aroused was to consider it in the light of future relations between the two countries. And the interpretation placed upon it was that it would be favourable to the British position. It was widely thought that the internal disorders in France would weaken her politically and militarily for a long time to come, and that afterwards, while she might be stronger as a power, she would be less likely to be in the mood to undertake the aggressive wars that she had formerly fought under her previous absolute monarchical rulers. Early in 1790 the Younger Pitt showed that he shared this outlook when he said, 'The present convulsions in France must sooner or later terminate in general harmony and regular order, and though the fortunate arrangements of such a situation may make her more formidable, they may also render her less obnoxious as a neighbour.'

At first, as the early events of the Revolution - the storming of the Bastille, the abolition of the French nobility's feudal immunities and the establishment of a new constitutional monarchy - proceeded, the general reaction among the British people was to welcome them with sympathetic approval and even enthusiasm. Since the Glorious Revolution of 1688 nearly all classes and opinions in the country had united in praising the excellence of the British constitution, especially as it was contained in the Bill of Rights and the Toleration Act, and in asserting that it was responsible for the stable, peaceable government which it had brought the nation during the eighteenth century.

Burke thought that the British form of government was the most perfect in existence since it embodied 'those rules of Providence which are formed upon the known march of the ordinary Providence of God.' And such admiration of the British constitution was shared by distinguished French political thinkers, whose writings were to contribute towards the outbreak of the Revolution. Montesquieu (1689-1755) considered that the British parliamentary monarchy with its 'mixed constitution' was the best form of government for the European kingdoms of his day; and Voltaire (1694-1778) admired its unique political and religious freedom, the entry of the nobility into public life and the esteem (instead of official suspicion) accorded to thinkers and writers.

Such French political observers compared their own country unfavourably with what they observed in Britain. And, indeed, popular opinion in Britain had long considered France to be a notorious example of outworn tyranny and unfair privilege. The 'freeborn Britons' despised it as the land of 'Popery, wooden shoes and black bread.' Now, a century after the Glorious Revolution, it seemed that the French were at last seeking to emulate it and attain a parliamentary system in their country. The philosopher, Jeremy Bentham, sent a plan of legal reform to the Comte de Mirabeau, the first of the revolutionary leaders to form a policy, which included the abolition of privilege and inequality and the establishment of a constitutional monarchy.

At the outbreak of the French Revolution, Britain had enjoyed six years of peace after the end of the American War of Independence. Pitt's fiscal reforms were starting to take effect, and country appeared to be recovering from the financial strains of the American War. It appeared as if Britain might be in a position to join with France in bringing a new tranquillity and stability to Europe.

Writers and poets especially welcomed the coming of the French Revolution, believing that the powerful example of France would spread the great ideas of 'liberty, equality and fraternity' to other countries and so mark the beginning of a

new age of happiness for all mankind. William Blake (1757-
1832) assumed a red cap of liberty when he walked about
London; and Robert Burns (1759-1796), then an excise officer,
sent firearms to the Revolutionary Convention in Paris. The
youthful William Wordsworth (1770-1850) went himself to Paris
and rejoiced at:

> 'France standing on the top of golden hours
> And human nature seeming born again.'

Robert Southey (1774-1843) recalled in 1824 how on the
outbreak of the Revolution 'old things seemed passing away,
and nothing was dreamt of but the regeneration of the human
race;' and Samuel Taylor Coleridge (1772-1834), while still a
schoolboy, wrote verses on the fall of the Bastille.

The effect of the events in France was also important in
British politics. The parliamentary opposition to Pitt's
ministry was aroused. Its leaders were ready to put
themselves at the head of a popular movement in favour of
political liberty. Charles James Fox, after perusing a few
newspapers, wrote of the fall of the Bastille, 'How much the
greatest event it is that ever happened in the world! and how
much the best!' And later he described the new French
constitution of 1791, which limited the authority of the
monarchy and deprived the Papacy of its power over the French
Church, as 'the most stupendous and glorious edifice of
integrity in any time or country.' And, though he had dressed
most carefully in his early days, he adopted a new style of
negligence in his attire to show his sympathy with the
democratic doctrines of the Jacobins, the most uncompromising
group among the French revolutionaries.

Outside Parliament, the Revolution was acclaimed with
particular enthusiasm by the Radicals, the members of the
various associations that were hostile to the existing system
of government and desired thoroughgoing reform. These had
come into being during the middle years of the eighteenth
century, but the general satisfaction with the established
constitution had not been favourable to their cause. The
outbreak of the French Revolution, however, gave them new
encouragement. The year 1791 saw the revival of the Society
for Promoting Constitutional Reform, which had been founded
in 1780 to obtain an enlarged franchise and shorter
parliaments, but had suspended its activities since 1784.

This was supported by other societies, some newly-founded
and including among them several formed to celebrate the
centenary of the Glorious Revolution, the best-known of them
being the London Revolution Society. The membership of these
British societies was, however, still largely from 'men of
rank and consequence' - idealistic or eccentric noblemen,
rationalist middle-class intellectuals, businessmen tired of
royal and aristocratic misgovernment and Dissenters, whose
civil disabilities, consequent upon their rejection of
membership of the Church of England, made them among the most
insistent upon political reform.

In November 1789 the London Revolution Society gathered in
a dissenting meeting-house to commemorate the landing of
William of Orange in England and heard a sermon by the
veteran Unitarian minister, Richard Price (1723-1791), which
was later printed as <u>A Discourse on the Love of our Country</u>
together with a congratulatory address from the Society to

the National Assembly set up at Versailles earlier that year
to initiate reform in France. Price described the French
Revolution as fulfilling the principles of the Glorious
Revolution. On that occasion the British had secured the
right 'to choose our own governors; to cashier them for
misconduct; and to frame a government for ourselves.' Now the
French were doing the same, and oppressors everywhere must
tremble and 'consent to the correction of abuses.'

This Discourse encouraged the reforming societies to urge
the relevance of the French revolutionary ideas to domestic
politics, and the London Revolution Society initiated a
friendly correspondence with the French revolutionary
societies, which was to continue until February 1792. Burke
was provoked to answer Price by publishing his Reflections on
the Revolution in France the next year. Beginning as an
attack on the English revolutionary societies, this went on
to consider the nature of the French Revolution in general.
Burke insisted that it was not an extension of the aims of
the Glorious Revolution to the rest of Europe, but rather a
bid to remould the European political structure in the light
of a false theory of human nature, which would be fatal to
what he regarded as the twin foundations of ordered society -
religion and landed property. He warned also that its
imposition would be attempted by force and violence, and
cruelty and bloodshed would be the inevitable result of the
movement.

The publication of the Reflections was accompanied by a
tearful and public rift between Burke and Fox in the House of
Commons in April 1791, but the immediate political effect of
the book was slight. The opposition were sufficiently united
to be able to make a serious challenge to Pitt over the
Ochakoff crisis when he had to withdraw humiliatingly his
demand that Russia should abandon its occupation of this
Black Sea port. The publication in August of Burke's Appeal
from the Old to the New Whigs, in which he attacked the
Foxites who supported the Revolution and urged those
supporting order and established authority to separate from
them, seemed likely to go unheeded.

By the time this book appeared, however, the French Church
was despoiled and emigre noblemen and priests were sailing
into Sussex ports in open boats, and Burke aided those
relieving the destitute exiles. People of 'substance and
respectability,' who remembered the Gordon Riots of June 1780
when London was at the mercy of a mob for six days, were
becomingly increasingly upset by the turn of events in France
- Louis XVI's unsuccessful flight to Varennes (June 1791)
followed by his imprisonment; the Paris massacres (September
1792); the execution of the King (January 1793); the Terror
(July 1793) - and what Burke called 'the proceedings of
certain societies in London.' His denunciation of the
destructive purposes of the Revolution aroused their
attention. Published at five shillings (25p.), it attained
the unprecedented sale of 32,000 copies in a year. By the end
of 1791, conservative Whigs, led by William Windham and Earl
Spencer, were advocating resistance to the French threat.

Burke was quickly answered by Radical writers. The most
able of the thirty-eight counterblasts which he aroused was
perhaps William Wordsworth's Letter to the Bishop of Llandaff

(1793), which was never published during the writer's lifetime (and later overtaken by a different outlook on his part -see no. 1175). The most influential and best-known critical reply to Burke was undoubtedly Thomas Paine's The Rights of Man (1790-1792), which secured him election as a deputy of the Convention in Paris. It was a masterly tract written in language which artisans and small shopkeepers could understand. It was a turning-point in the reform movement together with the formation of the London Corresponding Society in January 1792 with a membership drawn mainly from lower middle-class and working-men, who were organized in 'sections' throughout the country and exchanged 'constitutional information' by correspondence.

This soon led, however, to the establishment of opposing organizations, typical of these being the Association for the Support of the Laws and Liberties of the Country formed in December 1792 at the town of Horncastle in Lincolnshire, which declared itself 'perfectly satisfied with the Legislative Government of this Kingdom.' At the same time, action was taken against those who uttered 'seditious words.' Also in Lincolnshire a man, who said 'that he would plant the tree of liberty in England,' was sentenced to 'one year's imprisonment and to be privately whipped.'

The anti-revolutionary movement gained control of the nation, partly through such measures, but also because, despite its energy and enthusiasm, the reform movement attracted only a very small minority even of the working-class, which remained largely indifferent to its ideas and were ready to share with the governing classes the prevailing dread of French excesses and aggressive designs and to accept the growing likelihood of war against France. The spirit of patriotism among the British people came to outweigh the grievances that many of them felt.

By the end of 1792 the French government had made that war more likely by opening the River Scheldt to navigation in defiance of the Treaty of Utrecht of 1648, and Pitt, though believing that it would not be in Britain's interest to become embroiled in a European conflict, was making preparations for hostilities. Early the nest year France declared war on Britain, and Pitt formed an anti-French alliance, the First Coalition. Without accepting entirely Gladstone's judgement upon him (see no. 1179), Burke must share a large part of the responsibility for the attitude adopted in the country towards the Revolution and its consequences, but nevertheless the conflict was probably made inevitable by the warlike enthusiasm of the extremists in France.

570. Albert Mathiez, La Revolution Francaise et les Etrangers (Paris, 1919).

571. F. O'Gorman, The Whig Party and the French Revolution (Macmillan, 1967.

572. Alfred Cobban, 'Historians and the Causes of the French Revolution,' Aspects of the French Revolution (Paladin, 1968), pp. 29-33 [the passage about Burke].

573. Albert Sorel (trans. Alfred Cobban & J.W. Hunt), <u>Europe and the French Revolution</u> (Fontana, 1969).

574. Albert Goodwin, <u>Friends of Liberty: The English Democratic Movement in the Age of the French Revolution</u> (Hutchinson, 1979).

575. Robert R. Dozier, <u>For King, Constitution and Country: The English Loyalists and the French Revolution</u> (University Press of Kentucky, 1983).

576. T.W.C. Blanning, <u>THe Origins of the French Revolutionary Wars</u> (CUP, 1986).

577. Peter Burley, <u>Witness to the Revolution, American and British Commentators in France 1788-1794</u> (Weidenfeld & Nicolson, 1989).

578. H.T. Dickinson (ed.), <u>Britain and the French Revolution</u> (Macmillan, 1989).

579. William Doyle, <u>The Oxford History of the French Revolution</u> (OUP, 1989).

580. Simon Schama, <u>Citizens: A Chronicle of the French Revolution</u> (Viking, 1989).

Places Associated with Burke

William Hazlitt wrote in 1830 [A.R. Waller & Arnold Glover
(eds.), The Collected Works of William Hazlitt (Dent, 12 vols.,
1902-1906), vol. XII, p. 132], 'As I look down Curzon Street or
catch a glimpse of the taper spire of South Audley Chapel or
the family arms on the gate of Chesterfield House, the vista of
years opens to me, and I recall the period of the triumph of
Mr. Burke's Reflections on the French Revolution and the
overthrow of the Rights of Man.'
   Though Chesterfield House was demolished in 1937, the Chapel
(c. 1730) and enough eighteenth-century houses   remain in
Curzon Street and South Audley Street to-day to make possible a
repetition of Hazlitt's experience in this part of London. And
a similar value, despite peacetime development and wartime
destruction in London and elsewhere, is still attached to the
places and their surroundings known to Burke.

        *   *   *   *   *   *   *   *

581. NO. 12 ARRAN QUAY, DUBLIN.

   This was the house in which Burke was born. Arran Quay, laid
out about 1680, lies between Inns Quay and Ellis Quay in northwestern Dublin, 'where [the River] Liffey rolls his dead dogs
down to the sea,' as Burke wrote in 1744 (SA, pp. 1, 292). It
was because this area was constantly liable to flooding from
the River, which was considered unhealthy for him, that he was
sent away at a very young age to County Cork.

582. MONANIMMY CASTLE, CASTLETOWNROCHE, CO. CORK.

While   spending   his   early   childhood   with   his   maternal
grandfather in Ballyduff, Burke received his first education
in a village school at Castletownroche. It was held in the
ruins of Monanimmy Castle, which still survive on the northern
bank of the Blackwater.

583. TRINITY COLLEGE, DUBLIN.

By the time Burke was at the College (1744-1749), a grand
reconstruction and extension of its buildings had begun, so
that little survives of those which he knew as a student
there. The great Library, however, had been rebuilt between

1712 and 1732 and remains to-day very much the same since the time when he 'spent three hours in it every day' (JP, p. 14).
Burke did not go into residence in the College until he became a Scholar 1746. Its earliest Register of Chambers does not begin until 1780, but there is a tradition that his rooms were in no. 28 in the Library Square. This building was demolished in 1900 to make room for the Graduates Memorial Building.

584. SOUTH GREAT GEORGE'S STREET, DUBLIN.

This was the name later given to George's Lane where 'The Club,' of Trinity College met. It was a debating society founded in 1747 by Burke. [A.P.I Samuels, Early Life, Correspondence and Writings of Burke, p. 226; John Thomas Gilbert, History of Dublin (3 vols., Dublin 1861), vol. III, chap. iii].

585. MIDDLE TEMPLE, LONDON.

The late-seventeenth Gate House, the main entrance to the Middle Temple from Fleet Street, is still as it was known to Burke when he enrolled there in 1747, but some of the buildings beyond were badly bombed during the Second World War and have been replaced. The Honourable Society of the Inner Temple has a painting, after the style of Samuel Scott (1702-1772), showing the Middle Temple Hall and Fountain Court during Burke's time.
The Hall, completed in 1573, has been well restored. In it Burke would have gathered with other students to debate a topic under the guidance of a senior barrister known as a Reader. Oliver Goldsmith had chambers in No 2 Brick Court, and Burke is said to have wept there when visiting him on his death-bed in 1774.

586. GRECIAN COFFEE HOUSE, DEVEREUX COURT, STRAND, LONDON.

Devereux Court was built in the late seventeenth century on the site of Essex House, the mansion of Robert Devereux, Earl of Essex. The Grecian Coffee House, which is said to have taken its name from an early owner called Constantine, stood at no. 19 and was depicted by George Shpherd in a watercolour (1809). It particularly attracted playwrights and theatrical critics. Burke frequented it during his early years in London, when he was a member of the Middle Temple and also took part in the debates of the Robin Hood Society which met there. This was largely attended by 'gentlemen of the law,' students from the Temple seeking to gain experience in public speaking, and Burke first displayed his gift of eloquence there. The Club closed in 1843, when the building was remodelled and is now an inn called the Devereux. [See The History of the Robinhood Society, in which the Origin of that Illustrous Body of Men is Traced ... the Memoirs of the Various Members that Compose it are Given (1764)].

587. DICK'S COFFEE HOUSE, FLEET STREET, LONDON.

Situated near Temple Bar, this was also called Richard's after
Richard Torvor or Turver, who opened it in 1680 and was its
first owner. Burke wrote in a letter in 1747 describing
an escape from death or serious injury, 'As I sat in a house
under Dick's Coffee House, the back house, which joined it,
fell and buried Pue, the coffee house keeper, and his wife in
the ruins.' [JP, p. 31]. It became a French restaurant in
1885 and was demolished several years afterwards.

588. THE POPE'S HEAD, LONDON.

Joseph Emin, Autobiography (2nd. ed., Calcutta, 1918), pp. 89-
91, describes a meeting, probably late in 1755 or early in
1756, with Burke, who invited him to his rooms 'up two flights
of stairs, by the sign of Pope's Head, at a bookseller's near
the Temple.'

589. THE TULLY'S HEAD, PALL MALL, WESTMINSTER.

In the eighteenth century, Pall Mall was an unpaved roadway
between two royal residences - St. James's Palace and Carlton
House. The street was associated with chocolate houses, taverns
and clubs and also some shops. In 1735 Robert Dodsley (1703-
1764) opened a bookseller's shop at the Tully's Head, the site
of which is now number 52 and occupied by modern apartments.
Here he published Burke's Vindication of Natural Society and
The Sublime and Beautiful as well as the Annual Register with
Burke as its Editor (see no. 380).

590. CIRCUS HOUSE, BATH.

This was the residence of Dr. Christopher Nugent, an Irish
physician, with whom Burke lodged as both guest and patient in
1756 and whose daughter he married. It forms the north end of
the eastern segment of the Circus, which was designed by the
local architect, John Wood the Elder, and built in the years
following his death in 1754. Although the house is part of the
Circus, entry to it is through a doorway in Bennett Street, one
of the three streets leading into the Circus. A water-colour
drawing made in 1773 by Samuel H. Grimm shows the original
appearance of the Circus with its broad pavement ringed by
tethering-posts and mounting-steps and a roadway of cobbles
radiating from the covered resevoir in the centre, upon which
there were three iron lampholders.

591. WIMPOLE STREET, LONDON W.1.

After his marriage in 1757, Burke lived in the village of
Battersea, but the next year had a London home in this street,
which was built about 1724, as part of the Grosvenor Estate
laid out by John Prince, and still retains most of its plain
Georgian buildings. It is not always possible to identify a
particular house in which Burke lived because he often placed
only the street at the head of his letters. The

numbering of houses began in London and Westminster in 1735, but was only adopted slowly, and by the end of the eighteenth century there were still many houses which bore no number.

592. HILL STREET, MAYFAIR, LONDON W.1.
593. MONTAGU HOUSE, NO. 22 PORTMAN SQUARE, LONDON W.1.

Building began in Hill Street from 1745, and here Mrs. Elizabeth Montagu (1720-1800), authoress and leader of society, sought to make her husband's house 'the central point of union' for all the intellect and fashion of London. The intellectual ladies with her became known as 'Blue Stockings' because they preferred blue woollen stockings to the formal black silk, and she was soon called the 'Queen of the Blue Stockings.' Burke's writings and editorship of the Annual Register led him to be invited as a regular visitor to her 'Evenings,' which were 'conversation-parties' for the discussion of literary and topical subjects, and 'news' was his passport to her [CEB, vol. I. p. 171]. Some of the houses in the street still survive in altered form.
    In 1782 Mrs. Montagu moved to a new house Montagu House - designed for her at the north-west corner of Portman Square in Marylebone, then on the outskirts of the town. One of the rooms was painted with jasmine, roses and cupids, and another was adorned with the feathers of brightly coloured birds (C.S. Sykes, Private Palaces (Viking Penguin, New York, 1985), pp. 219-227). In December 1791 Mrs. Montagu entertained here Burke and the refugee Abbé Foullon, who had been a councillor-clerk in the Grande Chambre of the Parlement of Paris [CEB, vol. VI, p. 129); R. Blunt (ed,), Mrs. Montagu, Her Letters and Friendships (2 vols., 1923, vol. II, p. 252]. The house was destroyed by bombing in the Second World War. Only the gate-piers survived and have been re-erected in the grounds of Kenwood House, Hampstead Lane, London NW. 3. The Portman Inter-Continental Hotel stands on the site.

594. GARRICK'S VILLA, HAMPTON COURT ROAD, HAMPTON, MIDDLESEX

Built in the first half of the seventeenth century, the house was acquired in 1754 by Garrick, who lived in it until his death. It was enlarged for him by Robert Adam, who also designed the river-front with its portico and pillars. Burke often attended his parties there, which were famous, and when inviting Garrick and his wife to stay with him at Beaconsfield, he said that if they cared to bring their 'neighbour the Thames' with them it would be 'quite agreeable. After Garrick's death, it was later renamed Garrick's Villa and was divided into apartments in 1922, but it is much as when Burke knew it, including the paintings and carvings on the walls.

595. NO. 37 LEICESTER SQUARE, LONDON W.C. 2.

Originally Leicester Fields, Leicester Square was laid out in 1670 by the Earl of Leicester with handsome houses modelled upon those in Pall Mall. Joshua Reynolds bought this house on the west side and lived there from 1760 until his death in 1792. He added to it a fine gallery for the exhibition of his pictures and a large room for his sitters, among whom was Burke (see nos. 644-646). The site is now covered by the building of the Automobile Association.

596. HOUSE OF COMMONS, WESTMINSTER.

From 1547 until the fire of 1834, St. Stephen's Chapel within the Palace of Westminster was the chamber of the House of Commons and is now the site of St. Stephen's Hall there. In 1692 Sir Christopher Wren made alterations to it and after the Act of Union in 1707 built galleries to accommodate the forty-five Scottish members. Visitors came also to sit in the new galleries, and in 1778 Burke supported this practice, saying that it was 'the channel of information for the constituents of members,' 'a school for the instruction of youth' and 'the source of information and amusement to the ladies' (PD, vol. VII, p. 325). Another time a member protested when he saw David Garrick among them, saying that it was improper for players to listen to debates, but he was opposed by Burke, who insisted with Fox's support that parliamentary eloquence owed much to the stage and that Garrick was a great master of eloquence [Felix Barker and Peter Jackson, London (Cassell,1974), p. 171]. Paintings of the interior of the House by Peter Tillemans (1710) [Department of the Environment] and Karl Anton Hickel (1793) [National Portrait Gallery] show it was throughout Burke's membership.

597. QUEEN ANNE STREET, LONDON W.1.

Built from 1723 onwards, most of its original houses remain unspoiled. Burke lived here from 1762 to 1767 with Dr. Christopher Nugent, his father-in-law, who remained in the house after Burke moved (see no. 832).

598. BROOK'S CLUB, NO. 60 ST. JAMES'S STREET, WESTMINSTER.

Founded in 1764, Brook's Club met at Almack's Assembly Rooms in Pall Mall until 1778 when it moved to its present building, which is depicted in T. Rowlandson and A.C. Pugin, The Microcosm of London (1808). Its membership included many important Whig politicians, among them being Burke, Fox and Sheridan. Burke was elected a member in March 1783 on the proposal of the Duke of Devonshire. The dandies there laughed at his large spectacles, ill-fitting brown coat and bob-wig; and the outbreak of the French Revolution led him to oppose the views of most of the members. Fox, who gambled in the Great Subscription Room (still unchanged), was a favourite of twenty or thirty young Foxites - Members of Parliament and of the Club - whom Burke resentfully called Fox's 'light troops.' (CEB, Vol. VI, p. 273; SA, pp. 219, 225).

599. CHARLES STREET, ST. JAMES'S SQUARE, LONDON W.1.

Built from about 1745 onwards, some of the original substantial houses in the street still survive. Burke lived here from 1767 to 1769 and again from 1779 to 1785 (see no. 832). His usual practice throughout his political career seems to have been to take short leases, often for the winter, on houses in London, which were conveniently near to Parliament and the taverns and

other places he frequented. From 1768 onwards, he lived in his
prevailing town house while Parliament was sitting and at
Beaconsfield when it was not.

600. BUTLER'S COURT, (OR GREGORIES), BEACONSFIELD, BUCKS.

Situated about a mile from Beaconsfield, this mansion, erected
by Mistress Martha Gregory (died 1704), was bought by Burke
(together with six hundred acres of land) in 1768 and partly
rebuilt by him. After his death his widow lived there until her
death in 1812. It then became a school, but was burnt down in
1813. It was built upon the plan of Buckingham House, London
(which eventually became Buckingham Palace) with a grand centre
connected to wings by corridors. There is a description of it
in E.S. Roscoe, Betwixt Thames and Chilterns (Faber), chapter
VI, and an illustration in Peter Burke, Life of Burke, p. 101,
PM, facing p. 42 and S SA, between pp. 140 and 141 (see nos.
836-838). The site is now completely overbuilt by Beaconsfield
New Town, which grew around the railway station in the mid-
nineteenth century.

601. THE THATCHED HOUSE TAVERN, ST. JAMES'S STREET, LONDON.

From about 1705 this was a fashionable tavern, which was
frequented by Jonathan Swift. From 1769 Burke and other members
of the Opposition attended a series of dinners there before
Parliament reassembled and at various other times, usually on
Thursday evenings. Its site is now occupied by the Conservative
Club.

602. FLUDYER STREET, WESTMINSTER.

Burke lived between 1771 and 1772 in Fludyer Street, which was
a short street of twenty houses off Whitehall, south of and
parallel with Downing Street. It does not now exist, the
Foreign Office having been built over it in 1868. [Richard
Horwood, Map of London (1799), C.3.]

603. BROAD SANCTUARY, WESTMINSTER.

This is the open area in front of Westminster Abbey. In 1772
Burke lived on its south side in the old house of Dr. William
Markham, Headmaster of Westminster School. It was demolished in
1854 and replaced by the present block of stone-faced offices
(see nos. 862-864).

604. COVENT GARDEN THEATRE, WESTMINSTER.

The area of Covent Garden was once a produce garden belonging
to Westminster Abbey (or Convent). After the dissolution of the
monasteries, it was granted by the Crown to John Russell, first
Earl of Bedford. The fourth Earl (later first Duke) in 1630
promoted the building of a fashionable, aristocratic
residential square with a large open courtyard.
    In 1656 the Duke also established a market in the square,
which changed its character as shown by William Hogarth in his
engraving Morning, part of The Four Times of the Day (1738).
Coffee houses were opened, the best-known being the Bedford,

which was patronized by Burke together with Goldsmith, Boswell, Garrick and Sheridan and other of his friends. In 1732 John Rich opened the splendid, luxurious Covent Garden Theatre for both plays and operas, which was commemorated by Hogarth's cartoon Rich's Glory (1732). Burke often went there 'sitting in the best place' with his friends; and in 1773 when Goldsmith's She Stoops to Conquer had its premiere there, its author was so worried that he brought the members of the Literary Club to clap. The present theatre was built on the same site in 1858.

605. THE BUSH INN, BRISTOL.

Burke's election-day celebrations took place here, and he made his speech of thanks to the assembled electors after the declaration of the poll in 1774 (see nos. 881-883). It stood in Corn Street, near the Guildhall, but was demolished in 1864, and the Wiltshire Bank (now absorbed in Lloyd's) was built on the site.

606. BLAISE CASTLE, HENBURY, AVON.

In 1774 Burke stayed in this eighteenth-century sham Gothic castle (four miles north-west of Bristol) with Richard Champion during the election campaign. He admired the view from the dining-room so much that it was afterwards called Burke's window. The entire estate was purchased by Bristol Corporation in 1926.

607. SOMERSET HOUSE, STRAND, WESTMINSTER.

Burke took a large part in securing the passing of an Act of Parliament in 1775 to authorize the rebuilding of the Tudor and Stuart royal palace, Somerset House, to accommodate government departments and academic societies. The architect appointed for the new building was William Robinson, Secretary of the Board of Works, whose utilitarian plan was disliked by Burke and others. Robinson, however, died in 1775 and was replaced by Sir William Chambers, the Surveyor General and a personal friend of King George III and Burke. He designed the present building, which Burke described as 'seeming to avert the wrath of God from the black city, full of avarice, passion and vice.' [L.M. Bates, Somerset House. Four Hundred Years of History (Frederick Muller, 1967)]. The building and its surroundings, as known to Burke, may be seen in the water-colour by Thomas Griffin (1775-1802), London: The Thames from Westminster to Somerset House (c. 1801) [British Museum].

608. NO. 26 EASTCASTLE STREET, LONDON W.1.

Known as Castle Street East until 1918, it was first rated in 1723 and named after a local inn. It is now full of wholesale dress show-rooms. From 1773 until his death in 1806, no. 26 was the home of James Barry, the eccentric Irish painter, whom Burke brought to London and introduced to Reynolds and other painters (see no. 647) He lived alone; the house became dirty and ruinous; and he lived on bread and apples and scarcely admitted any visitor. Burke, however, was an exception, and one evening Barry entertained him with many anecdotes accompanied by a steak from the nearby Oxford Market (demolished 1876) and

a pint of porter from the inn. Burke declared that he had
'never spent a happier evening in his life' (John Timbs, A
Century of Anecdote 1760-1860 (Frederick Warne, n.d.).

609. PAYMASTER-GENERAL'S OFFICE, WHITEHALL, LONDON S.W.1.

This was Burke's office during the brief periods in 1782 and
1783 when he was Paymaster-General of the Forces. Built in
1732-1733 by John Lane on the site of part of the old Horse
Guard's building, it contains a conference room on the ground
floor and is now the Parliamentary Counsel Office

610 & 611. NOS. 9 & 37 GERRARD STREET, SOHO, LONDON.

Gerrard Street was built between 1677 and 1685 on land
belonging to Charles, Lord Gerrard. The developer was Nicholas
Barbon, who erected many buildings in London after the great
fire of 1666. The houses at first had three substantial storeys
with garrets. At first an aristocratic street, it became known
for its coffee houses and taverns and for the writers and
artists living in it. No. 9, which now has an early nineteenth-
front and is divided into offices, was much larger than the
rest and became in the 1760's the Turk's Head Tavern where
Samuel Johnson and Joshua Reynolds founded the Literary Club.
It met there from 1764 to 1783, and Burke was among its first
members. James E. Doyle (1822-1892) painted a picture of
Boswell, Johnson, Reynolds, Garrick, Burke, Paoli, Burney,
Warton and Goldsmith at a meeting of the Literary Club, making
careful reference to contemporary portraits [F.E. Halliday,
Doctor Johnson and his World (The Viking Press, New York,
1968), p. 67].
      Burke lived at no. 37 Gerrard Street, which is now a
restaurant and has been altered. He headed his letters there
from March 1787 to February 1790 (see no. 995).

612. ST. JAMES'S COFFEE HOUSE, NO. 87 ST. JAMES'S STREET,
     WESTMINSTER.

Established in 1705, this from the start had the reputation of
being a Whig house. Burke, Garrick, Reynolds and Goldsmith were
regular attenders. Since neither William nor Richard Burke
could belong to the exclusive Literary Club, Burke initiated
another dining-club, which had a partly overlapping membership
and met here [Richard Cumberland, Memoirs (2 vols., 1807). vol.
I, p. 369; PM, pp. 75-76]. The house closed towards the end of
the eighteenth century, and the site is now rebuilt.

613. NO. 6 DUKE STREET, ST. JAMES'S, WESTMINSTER.

The building of the street was completed during the 1680's.
Burke moved from Gerrard Street there at Michaelmas 1790 and
remained there until the summer of 1794. It was the last London
house he rented. None of the original houses now remains.

614. NEROT'S HOTEL, NO. 23 KING STREET, LONDON S.W.1.

During the last period of his life, when he had no house in
London, Burke stayed in this hotel, established by John Nerot
in one of the principal houses of the street, which became one

of the most fashionable in the West End. The house was demolished in 1835 to make way for the St. James's Theatre, which in turn was demolished in 1958 and replaced by St. James's House.

615. CREWE HALL, FARNDON, CHESHIRE.

Towards the end of his life, Burke was entertained among her company here by Frances Crewe (d. 1818), the charming and celebrated Whig hostess, whom he called the 'incomparable Mrs. Crewe.' Subsequently extracts from his table-talk written down by Mrs.Crewe were printed (no. 230). The mansion was built by Inigo Jones; it was badly damaged by fire in 1866, but restored in conformity with the original design and is still essentially the Jacobean house at which Burke stayed.

616. CROMWELL HOUSE (or HALE HOUSE), BROMPTON

Burke rented this seventeenth-century villa in Brompton (now South Kensington) for his ailing son, Richard, during his last illness in 1794 in the vain hope that the country air might cure him. It was demolished in 1855, and its site is now covered by the crossroads where Cromwell Road passes through Queen's Gate, London SW 7. There is a description of it in H.B. Wheatley, London Past and Present (2 vols., London, 1891), vol. I, pp. 475-476, and an illustration in Peter Burke, Life ofBurke, p. 278 (see no. 162) and Mary Cathcart Borer, TwoVillages, The Story of Chelsea and Kensington (W.H. Allen, 1973), p. 84.

617. TYLER'S GREEN HOUSE, PENN, BUCKS.

Burke established here a school for the destitute sons   of French refugees in 1796. The house had belonged to Major Thomas Haviland (died 1784), who was married to Burke's niece, and was situated about three miles north-west of Beaconsfield. Following the Major's death, it was empty and leased by the War Office, whom Burke persuaded to allow him to use it for his purpose. After the restoration of the monarchy in France, the French government maintained the school until 1820. Two years later the house was sold by auction in lots, pulled down and carried away as building material.

618. NO. 11, NORTH PARADE, BATH.

In 1796 and again in 1797 Burke went to Bath for his health, staying in this house. North and South Parade were also designed by John Wood the Elder and built between between 1739 and 1748. Burke felt much better after his first visit, but gained no benefit from the second and returned home to Beaconsfield to die.

Speeches of Burke

Guides to the printed sources in which the speeches made by Burke in the House of Commons are to be found are:

619. John A. Woods, A Bibliography of Parliamentary Debates of Great Britain (House of Commons Library Document No. 2, Her Majesty's Stationery Office, 1956).

620. David Lewis Jones, Debates and Proceedings of the British Parliaments (House of Commons Library Document No. 16, Her Majesty's Stationery Office, 1986).

Burke's principal parliamentary speeches are to be found in these sources:

621. W. Cobbett (ed.), The Parliamentary History of England, from the Earliest Period to the Year 1803 (36 vols., London, 1806-1820).

622. John Debrett (ed.), The Parliamentary Register (66 vols., London, 1780-1803).

623. The Senator, or Clarendon's Parliamentary Reporter (28 vols., London 1790-1801)

Not until 1909, when the government took over the publication of Hansard, have there been strictly verbatim reports of parliamentary debates. Of the above, Cobbett is the best single source. Debrett's speeches are often full, but some were supplied by the Members themselves and revised when received. The reports in The Senator are sometimes the most reliable, but the speeches may be abridged.

Burke's speeches (in Parliament and elsewhere) are collected in:

624. The Speeches of the Right Honourable Edmund Burke in the House of Commons and in Westminster Hall (4 vols., vols., London 1816).

625. The Political Tracts and Speeches of Edmund Burke, Esq., (Dublin, 1777)

His speeches about the American and Irish questions are
contained in:

626. The Political Tracts and Speeches of Edmund Burke
     (Dublin, 1777).

627 F.G. Selby (ed.), On American Taxation, On Conciliation
     with America, The Letter to the Sheriffs of Bristol
     (1895).

628. Hugh Law (ed.), Burke's Speeches and Letters on American
     Affairs (Dent, Everyman's Library, 1911).

629. G.S. Dickson (ed.), Conciliation with America by Edmund
     Burke (Nelson, 1937).

630. Matthew Arnold (ed.), Burke's Speeches on Irish Affairs
     (1881). [see no. 358]

Most of his speeches were less effective when they were
delivered than when they printed as pamphlets. They are
listed here chronologically with the first date of
publication:

631. To the Electors of Bristol, November 1774.

632. At His Arrival at Bristol, December 1774.

633. On American Taxation, January 1775.

634. On American Conciliation, March 1775.

635. On a Plan of Public Oeconomy, February 1780.

636. On a Plan for Oeconomical Reformation, March 1780.

637. At the Guildhall in Bristol, November 1780.

638. On the Commercial Treaty, January 1787.

639. On the Abolition of the Slave Trade, May 1789.

640. On Mr. Fox's East India Bill, January 1784.

641. On the Nabob of Arcot's Debts, August 1785.

642. In Westminster Hall, December 1792.

Contemporary Portraits of Burke

In a correspondence with the painter, James Barry, in 1774 (CEB, vol. III, pp. 4-9), Burke stated, 'I have been painted in my life five times; twice in little and three times in large. The late Mr. Spencer [Gervase Spencer, d. 1763] and the late Mr. Sisson [Richard Sisson, d. 1767] painted the miniatures. Mr. Worlidge and Sir Joshua painted the rest. A picture of me is now painting for Mr. Thrale by Sir Joshua Reynolds.'

The following is what is known of the existing portraits of Burke:

643. Thomas Worlidge (1700-1766) [Dr. Brendan O'Brien, Dublin]. This is perhaps the early portrait mentioned by Burke in the above letter.

644. Sir Joshua Reynolds (1723-1792) [Fitzwilliam Museum, Cambridge]. An unfinished double portrait of Rockingham and Burke, which was probably painted as a companion piece to Van Dyck's portrait of Strafford and his Secretary at Wentworth. From the evidence of Reynold's Sitters' Book it seems to have been begun in 1766, and work on it discontinued some time the next year.

645. Sir Joshua Reynolds [Earl Fitzwilliam, Milton], This was painted in 1769, and there is a copy of it from the studio of Reynolds in the National Portrait Gallery, London.

646. Sir Joshua Reynolds [National Gallery of Ireland, Dublin]. Begun in 1773, it ultimately hung in the Thrale library at Steatham and was sold by Mrs. Piozzi in 1816. This is the portrait stated as being painted in 1774 by Burke in his letter.

647. James Barry (1741-1806) [Professor Denis Gwynn, University College, Cork]. This is believed to be the one commissioned by Dr. Richard Brocklesby in 1776. There is a miniature on ivory of Burke after Barry in the National Portrait Gallery.

648. John Jones (1745?-1797) made an engraved portrait of Burke in 1786 or early 1787, (presumably from the portrait by Romney for the Duke of Richmond 1776 - CEB, vol. III, pp.

237-8) in William Bellenden, <u>De Statu Libri Tres</u> (1787).   He made another engraving from same painting, which he published 1790. The original painting by Romney is not known to have survived, but a contemporary copy is now in possession of Churchill College, Cambridge; and there is a copy of Jones's engraving of 1790 in the National Portrait Gallery.

649. Thomas Hickey (fl. 1760-1790). [National Gallery of Ireland]. A double portrait of Burke and Fox.

650. T.R. Poole [National Portrait Gallery]. A wax medallion made in 1791.

651. John Opie (1761-1807) [National Trust, Knole, Sevenoaks, Kent]. A portrait painted for John Frederick Sackville, third Duke of Dorset, in 1792.

652. John Hoppner (1758-1810) [Public Theatre, Trinity College, Dublin]. In 1795 the Board of the College asked Burke 'to sit for his picture to be hung up in the College.' The portrait, which was unfinished when Burke died, was paid for and framed in 1801.

Caricatures of Burke

668. Agricultural History.

669. Albion.

670. Anglia.

671. Antioch Review.

672. Bodleian Library Record.

673. British Journal of Eighteenth-Century Studies.

674. British Journal for the History of Science.

675. Bulletin of the John Rylands Library.

676. A Burke Newletter [1959-1967]; Studies in Burke and His Times [1967-1979]; The Eighteenth Century: Theory and Interpretation [from 1979].

677. The Catholic Historical Review.

678. Cornhill Magazine.

679. Dublin Magazine.

680. Durham University Journal.

681. English Historical Review.

682. Etudes Anglaises.

683. Historical Journal.

684. Historical Reflections.

685. History of European Ideas.

686. History of Political Thought.

687. History ToDay.

662. Mary Dorothy George, English Political Caricature to 1792: A Study of Opinion and Propaganda (OUP, 1960).

663. Thomas Wright & Robert Harding Evans, A Historical and Descriptive Account of the Caricatures of James Gillray (Bohn, 1851).

664. Thomas Wright, The Works of James Gillray (Chatto & Windus, n.d.).

665. R.J.H. Douglas, The Works of George Cruickshank (Dryden Press, 1903).

666. E. B. Krumbhaar, Isaac Cruickshank (University of Pennsylvania Press, 1966).

667. H.M. Atherton, Political Prints in the Age of Hogarth: A A Study of the Ideographic Representation of Politics (OUP, 1974).

Periodicals

653. Mary Dorothy George, <u>Catalogue of Personal and Political Satires Preserved in the Department of Prints and Drawings in the British Museum</u> (London, 1938-1947, reprinted 1978).
The many caricatures of Burke are to be found among those listed and described in vols. II to VI.

654. M.D. George, <u>Hogarth to Cruickshank: Social Change in Graphic Satire</u> (1967).
A selection of satires from this period.

655. M. Duffy (ed.), <u>The English Satirical Print, 1600-1832</u> (6 vols., Cambridge, 1986).
Caricatures from the British Museum's collection of prints.

656. The 17,000 prints in the British Museum, from all periods, can be had in microfilm published by Chadwyck-Healey, Ltd., Cambridge, 1978).

657. John Brewer (ed.), <u>The Common People and Politics, 1750-1790</u> (Chadwyck-Healey, Cambridge, 1986).
658. H.T. Dickinson (ed.), <u>Caricatures and the Constitution, 1760-1832</u> (Chadwyck-Healey, Cambridge, 1986).
Some of the prints dealing with Burke are reproduced in these two publications.

659. The Morgan Library in New York possesses Sir Robert Peel's valuable political caricatures from this period. It is contained in twelve folio volumes, one of which is completely devoted to Burke.

Further relevant books are:

660. Thomas Wright, <u>Caricature History of the Georges</u> (1868) [First published in two volumes as <u>England under the House of Hanover</u> (1848)].

661. George Paston (pseudonym of Emily Morse Symonds), <u>Social Caricature in the Eighteenth Century</u> (1905).

688. History Workshop.

689. Huntingdon Library Quarterly.

690. Journal of the History of Ideas.

691. Journal of the History of Philosophy.

692. Journal of Modern History.

693. Literature and History.

694. Massachusetts Review.

695. Modern Language Notes.

696. New Scholasticism.

697. Notes and Queries.

698. Philological Quarterly.

699. Political Science Quarterly.

700. Political Science Reviewe.

701. Political Theory.

702. Proceedings of the British Academy.

703. Publication of The Modern Language Association of America.

704. Quarterly Journal of Speech.

705. Review of English Studies.

706. Review of Politics.

707. Science and Society.

708. Society for the Study of Labour History Bulletin.

709. Southern Economic Journal.

710. Southwestern Social Science Quarterly.

711. The Times Literary Supplement.

712. Toronto University Quarterly.

713. Transactions of the Bristol and Gloucestershire Archaeological Society.

714. Transactions of the Royal Society of Canada.

715. The William and Mary Quarterly

Burke's Life and Career

SCHOOL, UNIVERSITY AND THE LAW (1729-1755)

716. PB, pp. 1-4.
717. JP, pp. 1-4.
718. RH, pp. 3-4.
719. SA, pp. 1-2.
720. T.H.D. Mahoney, Edmund Burke and Ireland, pp. 1-2.
     The Burke family.

721. R. Dunlop, Ireland from the Earliest Times to the Present Day (Humphrey Milford, 1922).
722. E. Curtis, A History of Ireland (Methuen, 1936).
723. C. Maxwell. Dublin under the Georges (Harrap, 1946).
724. C. Maxwell, Town and Country in Ireland under the Georges, 1714-1830 (Harrap, 1949)
725. H. Shearman, Anglo-Irish Relations (Faber, 1948).
726. J. Carty, Ireland: A Documentary Record 1607-1921 (Fallon, Dublin, 3 vols., 1949-1950)
727. H. Shearman, Ireland since the Close of the Middle Ages Harrap, 1955).
728. G. O'Brien, Anglo-Irish Politics in the Age of Grattan and Pitt (Dublin, 1988).
     The history of eighteenth-century Ireland and Anglo-Irish relations.

729. CEB, vols. I, pp. 1, 102-103hn; II, p. 413n; III, p. 99.
730. PB, p. 4.
731. JP, pp. 4-5.
732. RM, p.4.
733. SA, pp. 1-2.
734. T.H.D. Mahoney, Op. Cit., p. 1.
     Birth of Edmund Burke.

735. CEB, vol. I, p. 79n3.
736. PB, pp. 4-5.
737. JP, pp. 5-7
738. RM, pp. 5-8.
739. SA, p. 2.
740. T.H.D. Mahoney, Op. Cit., p.2.
     Early years.
741. Margaret F. Young, 'The Shackleton Letters,' The Kildare Archaeological Society Journal, vol. IX, no. 1, p. 73.

742. Mary Leadbeater, <u>Memoirs of Richard and Elizabeth
      Shackleton</u> (1849), <u>p. 2.</u>
743. <u>London Evening Post</u>, 14-17th. April 1770.
744. CEB, vol. I, pp. 3, 34, 124.
745. PB, pp. 5-8.
746. JP, pp. 7-12.
747. RM, pp. 8-21.
748. SA, pp. 2-3.
749. T.H.D. Mahoney, <u>Op. Cit.</u>, pp. 2-3.
  Schooldays at Ballitore.

750. CEB, vol. I, pp. 1-103.
751. PB, pp. 9-11.
752. JP, pp. 12-31.
753. RM, pp. 22-56.
754. SA, pp. 3-9.
755 T.H.D. Mahoney, <u>Op. Cit.</u>, pp. 3-4.
756. A.P.I. Samuels, <u>Early Life, Correspondence and Writings
      of Edmund Burke</u>, pp. 20-159.
  Student days at Trinity College, Dublin.

757. WEB, vol. I, p. 407.
758. CEB, vol. i, p. 111.
759. JP, pp. 31-32.
760. RM, pp. 57-58.
761. SA, pp. 8-10.
  At the Middle Temple.

762. Laetitia Matilda Hawkins, <u>Memoirs, Anecdotes, Facts and
      Opinions</u> (1814).
763. Donald C. Bryant, <u>Edmund Burke and his Literary Friends</u>
      p. 197.
764. Thomas W. Copeland, <u>Edmund Burke</u>, p. 46.
  Miss Laetitia Hawkins, daughter of Sir John Hawkins, Dr.
Johnson's friend and biographer - 'The Burkes, as the men of
that family were called, were not then what they were
afterwards considered, nor what the head of them deserved to
be considered for his splendid talents: they were, as my
father termed them, "Irish Adventurers;" and came into this
country with no good auguries, nor any decided principles of
action. They had to talk their way in the world that was to
furnish their means of living.'

765. CEB, vol. I, p. 127hn; vol. IX, p. 470.
766. JP, pp. 55-56.
767. RM, pp. 82-85.
768. BL, Add. MSS. 22130, f.10.
769. SA, p. 16.
770. Austin Dobson, 'At Tully's Head,' <u>Eighteenth-Century
      Vignettes, Second Series</u> (OUP World's Classics, 1923),
      pp. 22-49.
771. D.C. Bryant, <u>Edmund Burke and His Literary Friends</u>, pp.
      89-297.
  Engaged by Robert Dodsley to edit <u>Annual Register</u>.

WRITER AND PAMPHLETEER (1756-1764)

772. JP, pp. 45-46.
773. PM, pp. 331-332.
774. SA, pp. 13-14.
   Burke's <u>Vindication of Natural Society</u>, 1756.

775. JP, p. 49.
776. PM, pp. 331-332.
777. RM, pp. 72-74.
778. SA, p. 14.
   Burke's marriage, 1757.

779. <u>Monthly Review</u> (May 1757).
780. Ralph M. Wardle, <u>Oliver Goldsmith</u> (University of
   Kansas Press, 1957), p. 76.
781. RM, pp. 69-70.
   Review by Goldsmith of Burke's <u>Origin of our Ideas of the
   Sublime and Beautiful</u>.

782. <u>Notes and Queries</u>, Sixth Series, vol. V. p. 274.
783. JP, p. 54.
784. SA, pp. 14, 34.
   Birth of his sons, Richard and Christopher, 1758.

785. SA, p. 17.
   Horace Walpole to Elizabeth Montagu, 22nd. July 1761 -
'... a young Mr. Burke, who wrote a book in the style of Lord
Bolingbroke [<u>A Vindication of Natural Society</u>] that was much
admired. He is a sensible man, but has not worn off his
authorism yet - and thinks there is nothing so charming as
authors and to be one - he will know better one of these
days.'

786. JP, p. 69.
787. SA. p. 15.
   Death of Burke's father, 1761.

788. CEB, vol. I, p. 164. Burke to William Gerard Hamilton,
   [March 1763] - 'I know that your business ought on all
occasions to have the preference, to be the first and the
last, and indeed in all respects the main concern. All I
contend for is, that I may not be considered as absolutely
excluded from all other thoughts in their proper time and due
subordination.'
   [In thanking his patron for securing him a pension on the
Irish Establishment, Burke insisted that his duties should
allow him to engage in his literary activities].

789. WEB, vol. I, p. 407.
790. RM, p. 26.
   Burke on George Grenville (who was a lawyer) - 'The law
is, in my opinion, one of the finest and noblest of human
sciences; a science which does more to quicken and invigorate
the understanding than all other kinds of learning put
together; but it is not apt, except in persons very happily
born, to open and to liberalize the mind in the same
proportion.'

MEMBER OF PARLIAMENT FOR WENDOVER (1765-1774)

791. JP, pp. 71-76.
792. RM, pp. 113-114, 117.
793. SA, p. 20.
794. CEB, vol. I, pp. 178-186.
Burke's quarrel with Hamilton and relinquishment of his pension, 1765.

795. New Monthly Magazine , vol. XIV, p. 283.
796. RM, p. 140.
797. SA, pp. 24-25.
Lord Verney's presentation of Wendover to Burke.

798. James Boswell, The Life of Dr. Johnson (Everyman Edition, 2 vols.), vol. I, p. 619.
Dr. Johnson to Sir John Hawkins on Burke's entry into Parliament - 'Now we who know Mr. Burke, know, that he will be one of the first men in the country.'

799. CEB, vol. I. p. 67.
800. Rosalind Mitchison, Essays in Eighteenth-Century History, p. 45.
Burke to Hely Hutchinson, n.d. (c. May 1765)- 'There never was a season more favourable for any man who chose to enter the career of public life' [Burke on the time of his political beginnings].

801. CEB, Vol. I, P. 211.
Burke to Charles O'Hara, 11th. July 1765 - 'I have got an employment of a kind humble enough; but which may be worked into some sort of consideration, or at least advantage; Private Secretary to Lord Rockingham, who has the reputation of a man of honour and integrity; and with whom, they say, it is not difficult to live.'

802. HMC, Charlemont MSS, Thirteenth. Report. Appendix 10 (2 vols., 1891), 'Lord Charlemont's Memoirs - Observations on Edmund Burke,'vol. I, p.148.
'This most aimiable and ingenious man was private secretary to Lord Rockingham, a situation which was procured for him by the just attestation of all who knew him in behalf of his worth and abilities.'

803. CEB, vol. I, p. 223.
804. SA, p. 25.
Burke to Charles O'Hara, 24th. December 1765 - 'This is only to tell you that yesterday I was elected for Wendover, got very drunk and this day have an heavy cold.'

805. CEB, vol. I, pp. 233-234.
806. SA, p. 26.
807. Dixon Wecter, 'David Garrick and the Burkes,' Philological Quarterly, vol. XVIII, pp. 369-370.
David Garrick to Burke, 18th. January 1766 - 'Last night I had the honour and pleasure of enjoying your virgin eloquence! I most sincerely congratulate you upon it.... I pronounce that you will answer the warmest wishes of your warmest friend.'

808. Horace Walpole, <u>Memoirs of the Reign of King George the III</u>, vol. II, p. 273.
    'There appeared in this debate a new speaker, whose fame for eloquence soon rose high above the ordinary pitch. His name was Edmund Burke ... an Irishman, of a Roman Catholic family, and actually married to one of that persuasion. He had been known to the public for a few years by his "Essay on the Sublime and Beautiful' and other ingenoius works; but the narrowness of his fortune had kept him down, and his best revenue had arisen from writing for booksellers.'

809. JP, pp. 88-89.
810. RM, pp. 144-145.
    Richard Burke to James Barry, 11th. February 1766 - 'Your friend [Burke] has not only spoke, but he has spoke almost every day; as to how I shall leave you to guess, only saying that to a reputation not mean before, he has added more than the most sanguine of his friends could have imagined. He has gained prodigious applause from the public and compliments of the most flattering kind from particulars; it will add to what I know you already feel on this occasion, to be told that amongst the latter, was one from Mr. Pitt, who paid it to him in the House in the most obliging manner and in the strongest terms.'

811. James Boswell, <u>op. cit.</u>, vol. I, p. 320.
812. RM, p. 120.
    Samuel Johnson to Bennet Langton, 9th. March 1766 - 'Burke is a great man by nature and is expected soon to attain civil greatness.'

813. CEB, vol. I, pp. 251-252.
814. SA, p. 29.
    Burke to Charles O'Hara, 23rd. April 1766 - 'Pitt came down and made a fine flaming patriotick speech, chiefly against any sort of personal connections; he means with any beside himself.'

815. BL, Add. MSS. 22358, f. 34.
816. RM, p. 132.
    Lord Buckinghamshire to Grenville, June 1766 - 'Lord Albemarle and Mr. Bourk (I think that is the name not of Lord Rockingham's right hand but of both his hands) evidently direct the wires which move our political puppets there.'

817. HMC, <u>Eighth. Report, O'Conor MSS.</u>, p. 483.
818. Rosalind Mitchison, <u>Essays in Eighteenth-Century History</u>, p. 69.
    Charles O'Conor to Dr. John Curry, 17th. November 1766 - 'Whatever side he [Burke] engages on ... his abilities will be conspicuous.'

819. Horace Walpole, <u>Memoirs of the Reign of King George III</u> (4 vols., 1894), vol. III, p. 273.
820. RM, p. 143.
    Horace Walpole on Burke's part in the discussion in Parliament about the Stamp Act, 1766 - 'There appeared in this debate a new speaker, whose fame for eloquence soon rose high above the ordinary pitch. His name was Edmund Burke

...an Irishman, of a Roman Catholic family, and actually married to one of that persuasion. He had been known to the public for a few years by his essay on The Sublime and Beautiful and other ingenious works; but the narrowness of his fortune had kept him down, and his best revenue had arisen from writing for booksellers.'

821. WEB, vol. I, p. 183.
The Short Account of the Late Short Administration (1766) - 'That administration was the first that proposed and encouraged public meetings and free consultations of merchants from all parts of the kingdom; by which means the truest lights have been received; great benefits have already been derived to manufactures and commerce, and the most extensive prospects are opened for further improvement.'

822. O'Hara MSS.
   Dr. Christopher Nugent to Charles O'Hara, 26th. November 1767 - 'Our friends live now in Charles Street, St.James's Square, where they have a good deal more elbow room and are much more convenient to St. Stephen's Chapel, which they attend every day, very devoutly.'
   Burke's removal from Queen Anne Street to Charles Street (see no. 599).

823. O'Hara MSS.
824. R.J.S. Hoffman, Edmund Burke, New York Agent, p. 422.
825. CEB, vol. I, p. 340.
   Burke to Charles O'Hara, 11th. December 1767 - 'Everybody congratulated me on coming into the House of Commons, as being in the certain road of a great and speedy fortune; and when I began to be heard with some little attention, every one of my friends was sanguine. But in truth I was never so myself. I came into Parliament not as a place of preferment, but of refuge; I was pushed into it; and I must have been a Member, and that too with some eclat, or be little worse than nothing.'

826. CEB, vol. II, p. 7. Burke to James Barry, 19th. July
   1768.
827. JP, p. 107.
828. SA, p. 34.
   Burke's purchase of Gregories, Beaconsfield (see no. 600).

829. CEB, vol. I, pp. 350-352.
830. JP, p. 106.
   Burke to Richard Shackleton, 1st. May 1768 - 'I have made a push with all that I could collect of my own and the aid of my friends to cast a little root in this country. I have purchased a house with six hundred acres of land in Buckinghamshire twenty-four miles from London, where I now am. It is a place exceedingly pleasant; and I propose, God willing, to become a farmer in good earnest.'

831. CEB, vol. II, pp. 165-7, 180, 212, 223, 231-233, 237,
   240, 247, 316-319.
832. SA, pp. 37-38.
   Burke's farming at Beaconsfield.

833. Arthur Young, The Farmer's Tour through the East of England (1770-1771), Letter 31.
    Young's visit to Burke at Beaconsfield.

834. CEB, vol. II, pp. 27-29. Rockingham to Burke, 31st. May 1769; Burke & Richard Burke, Senior, to Charles O'Hara, 1st. June 1769.
835. SA, pp. 32-36.
    Burke's losses in speculation in East India stock, 1769.
836. CEB, vol. II, pp. 31, 438, 443.
837. SA, p. 37.
    Burke to David Garrick, 15th. June 1769 - 'I make no apology for asking a favour from you, because you need make none to me for refusing it. I wish then, that you could let me have a thousand pounds upon my bond until this time twelvemonth. I shall at that time, possibly before, be able to discharge it and will not fail to do so.' [But he did fail].

838. CEB, vol. II, p. 77.
    Burke to Rockingham, 9th. September 1769 - 'America is more wild and absurd than ever.'

839. CEB, vol. II, p. 80n.
840. R.J.S. Hoffman, Edmund Burke,New York Agent, p. 450n.
841. SA, p. 41.
    William Burke to Charles O'Hara, 1st. October 1769 - 'Among others Ned spoke, but with great modesty, declaring that the smallness of his property and the shortness of his time in the County made it a reluctant thing for him to speak, but ... the fact is that everybody till he spoke was heard, well indeed, but patiently, but when he had done there was a thunder, and I who had kept myself in the crowd heard the fellows say, "damn it, he has explained it," and they all understood their grievances quite plain.' [The freeholders' meeting at Aylesbury to organize a county petition against the conduct of the King's ministers].

842. Edmund Burke, Thoughts on the Cause of the Present Discontents (1770), p. 10.
    The political situation during the years after the accession of George III to the throne in 1760 - 'Coming to the throne in the prime and full vigour of youth, as from affection there was a strong dislike, so from dread there seemed to be a general averseness, from giving anything like offence to a Monarch, against whose resentment opposition could not look for a refuge in any sort of reversionary hope.'

843. Catherine Graham Macaulay, Observations on a Pamphlet entitled, Thoughts on the Cause of the Present Discontents (Dilly, 1770).
    'We cannot help wondering at the corruptness of the heart and deception of the head of the same writer, who, whilst, he emphatically sets forth the tyranny growing from a trust too long continued to parliament, yet absolutely declaims against the quick return of power into the people's hands.'

844. Mrs. Paget Toynbee (ed.) The Letters of Horace
Walpole, fourth Earl of Orford (OUP, 16 vols., 1903-
1905), vol. VII, p. 378.
'Mr. Burke (Lord Rockingham's governor) has published a
pamphlet that has sown the utmost discord between that
faction and the Supporters of the Bill of Rights. Mrs.
Macaulay has written against it.'
   Comments made upon Burke's Thoughts on the Cause
of the Present Discontents by Catherine Macaulay (1731-1791),
sister of John Sawbridge, M.P., (c.1732- 1795), one of the
founders of the society of Supporters of the Bill of Rights.

845. R.J.F Hoffman, Edmund Burke, New York Agent, p. 468.
846. CEB, vol. II, pp. 139-40.
   Burke to Charles O'Hara, 21st. May 1770 - 'The Pamphlet,
which contains our Creed, has been received by the publick
beyond my expectations. The courtiers admit it to be a piece
of gentlemanlike honesty. The fiercest enemies it has yet met
with are the republican factions.'
   Burke on the reception accorded to   Thoughts on the Cause
of the Present Discontents.

847. CEB, vol. II, p. 213. Burke to Judge Robert R.
   Livingston, 9th. June 1771
848. Horace Walpole, Last Journals, vol. I, p. 494.
849. JP, pp. 130-131.
850. RM, pp. 216-218.
851. SA, pp. 69-70.
   Burke appointed Agent to the General Assembly of New York,
1771.

852. O'Hara MSS.
853. Ross J.S. Hoffman, Edmund Burke, New York Agent, p. 513.
854. CEB, vol. ii, p. 301n3.
   William Burke to Charles O'Hara, 2nd. February 1772 - 'Ned
is moved to the House Dr. Markham once lived in, near the
Abbey. It is convenient for the House of Commons, airy in
itself and very roomy. Mrs B[urke] has her two rooms, and Ned
his Study all upon one floor. Richard is in lodgings.' (see
no. 603).

855. J. Boswell, Life of Johnson, vol. I, p. 487.
   Oliver Goldsmith speaking to Boswell of Johnson, 10th. May
1773 - 'Is he like Burke, who winds into a subject like a
serpent?'

856. CEB, vol. II, pp. 517-518.
857. JP, pp. 140-141.
   Burke to General Charles Lee, 1st. February 1774 - 'When
one considers what might be done there [in America], it is
truly miserable to think of its present distracted condition.
But as the errors which have brought things into that state
of confusion are not likely to be corrected by any influence
of ours upon either side of the water, it is not wise to
speculate too much on the subject. It can have no effect but
to make ourselves uneasy, without any possible advantage to
the public.'

MEMBER OF PARLIAMENT FOR BRISTOL (1774-1780)

858. CEB, vol. II, p. 528.
    Burke to New York Assembly, 6th. April 1774 - 'Lord North has assumed a style of authority and more decision, and the Bill laying Boston under a commercial inderdict during the King's pleasure has been proposed and supported quite through, with expressions of the utmost firmness and resolution.'

859. Hugh Law (ed.), <u>Burke's Speeches and Letters on American Affairs</u> (Dent, Everyman's Library, 1911), p. 11.
    Burke's Speech on American Taxation, 19th. April 1774 - 'Would twenty shillings have ruined Mr. Hampden's fortune? No! but the payment of half twenty shillings, on the principle it was demanded, would have made him a slave.'

860. CEB, vol. III, pp. 33-34, 55-56.
861. JP, p. 150.
862. SA, p. 75.
    Lord Verney's inability to allow Burke to retain Wendover.

863. Hester Lynch Piozzi, <u>Anecdotes of the late Samuel Johnson</u> (1786).
864. RM, p. 236.
    Dr. Johnson's parting words to Burke before he set out to Bristol for the election - 'Farewell, my dear sir, and remember that I wish you all the success that ought to be wished you, by an honest man.'

865. CEB, vol. III, p. 3.
866. JP, pp. 151-152.
867. SAS, pp. 76-77.
    The Bristol Election, 1774.

868. Hugh Law, <u>op. cit.</u>, p. 66.
    Burke's speech at his arrival at Bristol before the election at that city, 1774 - 'The liberty, the only liberty I mean, is a liberty connected with order; that not only exists along with order and virtue, but which cannot exist at all without them.'

869. <u>Bristol Journal</u>, 5th. November 1774.
870. <u>SA</u>, p. 77.
    Henry Cruger, an American-born Bristol merchant and fellow Member for Bristol with Burke - 'It has ever been my opinion that the electors have the right to instruct their members.'

871. WEB, vol., p. 447.
872. P.T. Underdown, <u>Bristol and Burke</u>, p. 9.
873. Hugh Law, <u>op. cit.</u>, p. 73.
    Burke's speech of thanks to the electors of Bristol, 3rd. November 1774 - 'Parliament is not a congress of ambassadors from different and hostile interests;...but a deliberate assembly of one nation, that of the whole.... You choose a member indeed; but when you have chosen him,

he is not a member of Bristol, but he is a member of
Parliament.'

874. James Boswell, op. cit., vol. II, p. 269.
     Burke to Boswell - 'Though I have the honour to
represent Bristol, I would not like to live there; I should
be obliged to be so much upon my good behaviour.'

875. J.E. Norton (ed.), Letters of Edward Gibbon (Cassell,
     3 vols., 1956), vol. I, p. 45.
     Gibbon to J.B. Holroyd, 12th. December 1774 - 'Burke [in
Parliament] was a water-mill of words and images.'

876. Hugh Law, op. cit., p. 91.
     Burke's Speech on Conciliation with America, 22nd. March
1775 - 'England, Sir, is a nation which still I hope
respects, and formerly adored, her freedom. The colonists
emigrated from you when this part of your character was
most predominant, and they took this bias and direction the
moment they parted from your hands. They are therefore not
only devoted to liberty, but to liberty according to
English ideas and on English principles.'

877. CEN, vol. III, pp. 139-140 - Marquess of Rockingham to
     Burke; Richard Burke, Snr., to Richard Champion.
878. HMC, Charlemont MSS, vol. II, p. 391 - Henry Flood
     to James Caulfeild, First Earl of Charlemont.
879. JP, p. 156.
880. SA, p. 82.
     Comments upon Burke's Speech on Conciliation with
America.

881. CEB, vol. II, p. 51.
     Burke to Rockingham, 23rd. August 1775 - 'We know that
all opposition is absolutely crippled if it can obtain no
kind of support out of doors.'

882. Robert Bisset, Life of Edmund Burke, vol. II, p, 429.
883. C.B. Macpherson, Burke, pp. 21-22.
     Adam Smith's agreement with Burke, whom he met when
elected to the Literary Club in 1775 - He was the only man
who, without communication, thought on these topics as he
did.'

884. CEB, vol. II, p. 277.
     Burke to Richard Shackleton, 25th, May 1776 - 'As to
myself and the part I have taken in my time, I apprehend
that there was very little choice.'

885. CEB, vol. III, pp. 356-357.
     Burke to Richard Champion, 26th. June 1777 - 'Until I
knew it, both by my own particular experience and by my
observation of what happened to others, I could not have
believed how very little the local constituents attend to
the general line of conduct observed by their member. They
judge of him solely by his merits as their special agent.'

886. CEB, vol. III, pp. 380-388.
887. Stanley Ayling, Fox, p. 55.
    Burke to Charles James Fox, 8th. October 1777 - 'Do not be in haste. Lay your foundations deep in public opinion .... I do not know so sound a bottom to build on as our party ....I love that party very well and am clear that you are better able to serve [it] than any man I know.'

888. Hertfordshire Record Office, Baker Letters, no. 58.
889. CEB, vol. III, pp. 388-390.
    Burke to William Baker, 12th. October 1777 - 'Ill success, ill health, minds too delicate for the rough and toilsome business of our time, a want of stimulous of ambition, a degeneracy of the Nation, which they are not lofty enough to despise, nor skilful enough to cure, have, altogether, I am afraid contributed very much to weaken the spring of Characters, whose fault it never was to be too elastick and too firmly braced.'

890. HMC, Fourteenth Report, Appendix 1 (1894), p. 11.
    George Johnstone to [the Marquis of Granby], 29th. November 1777 - 'Burke attacked Wedderburn (the Attorney-General] with repeated flashes of wit like the forked glare of lightening in a thunderstorm under the line. He was shrivelled under it like a blooming tree after a hurricane.'

891. PR, vol. VIII, p. 374.
892. PD, vol. VIII, p. 30.
    Burke, during a debate in the House of Commons, on 13th. February 1778, 'in the warmth of his indignation, threw the book of estimates at the Treasury Bench; which, taking the candle on its way, had nearly struck Mr. Ellis's shins.' [Welbore Ellis, Treasurer of the Navy].

893. CEB, vol. III, p. 427.
    Burke to Richard Champion, 11th. April 1778 on the Earl of Chatham's collapse in Parliament when speaking against the granting of sovereignty to America - 'Lord Chatham fell upon the bosom of the Duke of Portland, in an apoplectick fit, after he had spit his last venom.'

894. T. Keppel, Life of Keppel (1842,), vol. II, pp. 3-4, 260.
895. Edward Pelham Brenton, Life of Earl St. Vincent (1838), vol. I, p. 24.
896. CEB, vol. IV, pp. 35-36, 42-43.
897. PH, vol. XIX, p. 730; XX, p. 64.
898. WEB, vol. V, p. 146.
899. Sir John Fortescue (ed.), Correspondence of King George III, 1760-1783 6 vols., 1927-1928), vol. IV, pp. 234-235, 280, 294-296, 340-341.
900. Earl of Albermarle, Memoirs of the Marquis of Rockingham (1852), vol. II, pp. 369-370.
901. JP, p. 178.
902. RM, pp. 266-268.
903. SA, pp. 88-89.
    The affair of Admiral Keppel, 1778.

904. Wentworth Woodhouse Muniments, R 140-149.
905. CEB, vol. IV, pp. 159-164.
     Rockingham to Burke, 3rd. November 1779 - 'It matters
not whether it has as yet been declared at the market cross
in every town in England, that the system of government has
misled and that the corrupt influence of the Crown has
enabled the Ministers to carry into execution the Measures
by which this Country has been ruin'd - I now believe that
the above is the general predominant opinion of the Nation,
and I think the meansof power and the means of corrupt
influence in the Crown must soon submit to be shorn. N.B. I
must prefer the shears to the Hatchet.'

906. CEB, vol. IV, pp. 226-229.
907. JP, pp. 185-186.
908. Herbert Butterfield, George III, Lord North and the
     People (1949), pp. 383-387.
     Burke to the Chairman of the Buckinghamshire Meeting for
Obtaining Parliamentary Reform, 12th. April 1780 - 'I will
not deny our constitution may have faults; and that those
faults, when found, ought to be corrected; but, on the
whole that constitution has been our own pride and an
object of admiration to all other nations.... There are
many things in reformation which would be proper to be
done, if other things can be done along with them; but
which, if they cannot be accompanied, ought not to be done
at all.'

909. Bonamy Dobree (ed.), The Letters of King George III
     (Cassell, 1935), p. 135.
     The King to Lord North, 19th. May 1790 - 'Lord North
cannot doubt that I received with pleasure his account of
Mr. Burke's [Economical Reform] Bill having been defeated
in the several clauses that were before the Committee
yesterday.'

910. HMC, Dartmouth MSS, Eleventh. Report, Appendix V
     (1887), p. 510.
911. CEB, vol. IV, pp. 241-243, 254-258, 263.
912. JP, pp. 188-191.
913. SA, pp. 97-98.
914. J. Paul de Castro, The Gordon Riots (OUP, 1926), pp.
     4, 21, 64, 65, 81, 164, 177.
915. Christopher Hibbert, King Mob (Longmans, Green, 1959),
     pp. 26, 36, 48, 54, 135.
     Burke and the Gordon Riots, June 1780.

916. CEB, vol. IV, pp. 337-339, 358-359; vol. V, pp. 59,
     208.
917. D.C. Bryant, Edmund Burke and His Literary Friends
     (1939), p. 182.
918. G. Crabbe, Life of the Rev. George Crabbe (1834), pp.
     90, 95, 187.
919. JP, pp. 291. 213, 475.
920. RM, pp. 174,259, 270, 295, 389.
921. SA, pp. 136, 150-152.
     Burke's befriending of George Crabbe.

922. Wentworth Woodhouse Muniments, R 140-144.
923. CEB, vol. IV, pp. 299-302.
     Burke to Lady Rockingham, 27th. September 1780 - 'If
there were any two objects upon which the people of England
had seemed to set their hearts for some time past, they
were the reduction of the influence of the Crown and the
shortening of the duration of Parliaments.'

924. WEB, vol. II, pp. 140, 145-148, 151-154; V, pp. 513-
     521
925. CEB, vol. III, 207-210, 318-321.
926. P.T. Underdown, Bristol and Burke (Bristol, 1961), pp.
     10-16.
927. RM, pp. 280-281.
928. SA, p. 98.
     Burke's disagreements with the electors of Bristol.

929. Edmund Burke, Speech at Bristol Previous to the
     Election (1780).
930. WEW, vol. II, p. 138.
931. SA, p. 98-99.
     'We...plunged back again to war and blood [in America];
to desolate and be desolated, without measure, hope or end.
I am a royalist, I blushed for the degradation of the
crown. I am a Whig, I blushed for the dishonour of
parliament. I am a true Englishman. I felt to the quick for
the disgrace of England. I am a man, I felt for the
melancholy reverse of human affairs, in the fall in the
first power in the world.'

932. Autobiography of Sir Samuel Romilly (1840), vol. I, p.
     213.
933. JP, pp. 193-194.
     Romilly to the Revd. John Roget - 'I am not surprised
that you so much admire Burke's speech [on American
taxation]; but though it is somewhat cruel to tell you so,
it is far inferior to some of his later compositions,
particularly to a speech made in Bristol at the last
election in justification of his own conduct, which is
perhaps the finest piece of oratory in our language.'

934. CEB, vol. X, pp. 325-326, 328-330.
935. WEB, vol. II, p. 171.
936. Gentleman's Magazine, vol. I, p. 618.
937. G.E. Weare, Burke's Connection with Bristol from 1774
     till 1780 (Bristol, 1894), pp. 147-166.
938. Ernest Barker, Burke and Bristol (Bristol, 1931, p.
     31.
939. P.T. Underdown, Bristol and Burke (Bristol, 1961), pp.
     16-17.
     Burke's withdrawal of his canditure at Bristol.

940. CEB, vol. IV, p. 282.
941. JP, pp. 196-197.
     Charles James Fox to Burke, 15th, September 1780 -
'Indeed, my dear Burke, it requires all your candour and
reverse of selfishness (for I know no word to express it)
to be in patience with that rascally city [Bristol].'

MEMBER OF PARLIAMENT FOR MALTON (1781-1794)

942. PM, p.317, n. 15.
943. John Norris, Shelburne and Reform (Macmillan, 1963),
     p. 6.
     Burke's opinion of Shelburne - 'He wants what I call
principles, not in the vulgar sense of a deficiency of honour
or conscience - but he totally wants a uniform rule and
scheme of life.'

944. James Boswell, Life of Samuel Johnson, vol. II, p.402.
     Burke's remark (1781) to Boswell, who had spoken of
Herbert Croft's Life of Dr. Young as a good imitation of
Johnson's style - 'No, no,' said he, 'it is not a good
imitation of Johnson; it has all his pomp, without his force;
it has all the nodosities of the oak without its strength; it
has all the contortions of the Sybil without the
inspiration.'

945. Edmund Burke, On Pitt's First Speech (1781).
     'Not merely a chip of the old "block," but the old block
itself.'

946. Edmund Burke, Letter to a Noble Lord (1796).
947. WEB, vol. V, p. 117.
948. RM, p. 189.
     Burke's opinion of Lord North - 'He was a man of admirable
parts; of general knowledge; of a versatile understanding
fitted for every sort of business; of infinite wit and
pleasantry; of a delightful temper; and with a mind most
perfectly disinterested. But it would be only to degrade the
memory of a great man, to deny that he wanted something of
the vigilance and spirit of command, that the time required.'

949. Milton MS.
950. PM, p. 125.
     Mrs. Burke to Richard Champion, 1st. January 1782 - Mr.
Burke has been full as busy since we came into the country as
he was in the town. He is trying whether we shall have more
success in saving the East than he had in his endeavours for
the West.... God's will be done.'

951. BL. Add. MSS. 34418, f. 10.
952. CEB, vol. IV, pp. 424, 428-429, 430, 434-435, 437; V,
     pp. 21-23.
953. Earl of Albemarle, Memoirs of the Marquis of Rockingham
     (1852), vol. II, pp. 116-117.
954. Lord Edmund Fitzmuarice, Life of the Earl of Shelburne
     (1875-1876), vol. II, pp. 49, 62.
955. Christopher Hobhouse, Fox (1964), pp. 115-116.
956. JP, pp. 215-218.
957. RM, pp. 219-301.
958. SA, pp. 110-117.
     Burke's first term as Paymaster-General, 1782.

959. PH, vol. XXI, pp. 33-34.
960. SA, p. 114.
961. Richard Pares, King George III and the Politicians
     (1953), p. 127.

Burke on sinecures - 'I would leave to the Crown the possibility of conferring some favours, which, whilst they are received as a reward. do not operate as corruption. When men receive obligations from the Crown through the pious hands of fathers ... the dependencies which arrive from thence are the obligations of gratitude and not the fetters of servility. Such ties originate in virtue, and they promote it.

962. Fitzwilliam MSS, Bk. 1170.
963. CEB, vol. V, pp. 19-21.
964. John Norris, op. cit., p. 172.

Burke to Lord Loughborough, 17th. July 1782 - To think that all the labours of his [Rockingham's] life, and that all the labours of my life, should in the very moment of success produce nothing better than the delivering of the Kingdom into the hands of the E. of Shelburne, the very thing (I am free to say to you and to everybody) the toils of a life ten times longer and ten times more important than mine would have been well employed to prevent.'

965. Statue of the Marquis of Rockingham at Wentworth Woodhouse, Yorkshire, by Joseph Nollekens and dated 1774.
Inscription by Burke - 'His virtues were his arts.'

966. CEB, vol. I, pp. 85, 86-91. 98, 99-100; VI, pp. 374-375.
967. JP, pp. 223-232.
968. RM, pp. 303-310.
969. SA, pp. 123-133.

Burke's second term as Paymaster-General, 1783.

970. CEB, vol. V, p. 120.
971. F. Darblay (Fanny Burney), Diary and Letters (ed. C. Barrett (4 vols., 1876), vol. I, p. 60.
972. Sarah Kilpatrick, Fanny Burney (David & Charles, 1980), p. 106.
973. SA, p. 143.

Burke in 1783 secured for Dr. Charles Burney the post of organist at the Royal Hospital, Chelsea - 'This is my last act in office.'

974. Thomas W. Copeland, Edmund Burke, Six Essays (Jonathan Cape, 1950), pp. 20-21.

Boswell's visit to Burke at Beaconsfield, 21st. April 1783 - 'The place looked most beautiful. He was at the window with a scratchwig and let me in. His hall was admirable, contained many busts.... I was affected with wonder by seeing a suite of rooms hung with valuable pictures in rich-gilded frames: seven Landscapes of Poussin which Sir Joshua values at £700, a fine Titian, a ------; in short a great many.'

975. Katherine C. Balderston (ed.), Thraliana (2 vols., OUP, 1942), vol. I, p. 475.

Mrs. Thrale's visit to Burke with her husband and Dr. Johnson - 'I lived with him and his lady at Beaconsfield among dirt, cobwebs, pictures and statues that would not have disgraced the city of Paris itself; where misery and

magnificence reign in all their splendour and in perfect
amity'.

976. A. Francis Steuart (ed.), <u>The   Last   Journals   of Horace
    Walpole</u> (2 vols., 1910), vol. II, pp. 453-456.
977. R.W. Ketton-Cremer, <u>Horace Walpole</u> (Methuen,   3rd.   ed.,
    1964), pp. 246-247.
    Walpole's indignation at Burke's attempt to obtain from
Sir Edward Walpole, for his own benefit, the lucrative
sinecure of the Clerkship of the Pells - 'Can one but smile
at a reformer of abuses reserving the second great abuse for
him self?'

978. HMC, <u>Fourteenth Report, Appendix 1</u> (1894), p. 97.
    Daniel Pulteney to the Duke [of Rutland], 25th. May 1784 -
'Pitt laughed at Burke very successfully for the awkward
irregular manner of introducing Irish attachments.'

979. James Boswell, <u>Life of Johnson</u>, vol. II, p. 603.
    Dr. Johnson's last words to Burke - 'I must be in a
wretched state, indeed, when your company would not be a
delight to me.'

980. J. Greig (ed.), <u>The Farington Diary</u> (8 vols.,   1922-
    1928), vol. I. p. 5.
    Mirabeau's visit to England, 1785 - 'It was very singular
to see Mirabeau and Burke in controversy. Mirabeau could
speak little English, Burke French imperfectly. Yet these
celebrated men argued with as much earnestness and
continuation as if they had been speaking in a language
common to both. Mirabeau was astonished with the eloquence
and force with which Burke expressed his meaning though he
could only do it by uniting words of different languages.'

981. HMC, <u>Fourteenth Report, Appendix 1</u> (1894), p. 199.
    The Earl of Chatham to the Duke [of Rutland], 13th. April
1785 - 'Mr. Burke seems determined not to let us have a short
session, as I had hoped. It is impossible yet to judge from
the catalogue of crimes he has given in, each of which is a
folio volume, whether anything really serious or only
vexation and consumption of time will be the consequence; but
I am afraid the prospect of the latter, at least, seems
inevitable, perhaps both. Should it end in nothing, I shall
hate him as much as he does Hastings.' [A debate on Ireland].

982. BL, MSS. 29219, Vol. I.
983. <u>Annual Register</u>, 1786, p. 94.
984. RM, p. 325.
    A note in the handwriting of Hastings about the enquiry by
John Scott, his agent, about his intention to charge him -
'1786. 24 January. Major Scott called on Mr. Burke to declare
whether he meant to make his charge and when. Mr. Burke
replied with a story of the Duke of Parma, who to a similar
demand of Henry IV answered, "that he had not travelled from
Amiens to Paris to learn from his enemy when and where was
the best day to fight him." In this decent and dignified way
was this great work begun.'

985. J.T. Smith, <u>A Book for a Rainy Day</u> (1845 ed.), p. 110.
    A description by the painter and antiquary, who lived in
Gerrard Street at the same time as Burke - 'Many a time when
I had no inclination to go to bed at the dawn of day, I have
looked down from my window to see whether the author of the
<u>Sublime and Beautiful</u> had left his drawing-room, where I had
seen that great orator during many a night after he had left
the House of Commons, seated at a table covered with papers,
attended by an amenuensis who sat opposite him.' [See no.
611].

986. HMC, <u>Dartmouth MSS, Eleventh Report, Appendix V</u> (1787,
    p. 472.
    Dr. John Ash to the Earl of Dartmouth, 4th. October 1787 -
'At Lord Loughborough's I met with Mr. Edmund Burke, and we
had a fine dish of politics, that continued near hours in
serving up. He is a wonderful man in abilities and reading,
but yet not to deprecate his excellencies, I have met with
men who have arranged their acquisitions with greater skill
and precision.'

987. <u>The Times</u>, 20th. February 1788.
988. <u>SEB</u>, vol. I, p. 231.
989. <u>Fitzwilliam Correspondence</u>, vol. III, p. 73.
990. <u>RM</u>, pp. 337-338.
    Burke's impeachment of Hastings.

991. Averyl Edwards, <u>Fanny Burney,1752-1840</u> (Staples Press,
    1948), pp. 85-86.
    Fanny Burney on the beginning of the proceedings - 'As the
doors were flung open, I saw Mr. Burke, as head of Committee
[of Management], make his solemn entry. He held a scroll in
his hand and walked alone, his brow knit with corroding care
and deep labouring thought - a brow so different to that
which had proved so alluring to my warmest admiration when I
first met him .... How did I grieve to behold him now, the
cruel Prosecutor (such to me he appeared) of an injured and
innocent man!'

992. J. Greig (ed.), <u>Farington Diary</u>, vol. III, p. 15.
993. Warren Derry, <u>Dr. Parr, A Portrait of the Whig Dr.
    Johnson</u> (OUP, 1966), p. 79.
    Parr's comment to Burke on his opening speech at the
impeachment of Hastings, 1788 - 'Your speech was oppressed by
epithet, dislocated by parathenthesis and debilitated by
amplification.'

994. Austin Dobson (ed.), <u>The Diary and Letters of Mme.
    D'Arblay</u> (6 vols., 1905), vol. III, p. 448.
    Fanny Burney on the speech - 'Nervous, clear and striking
was almost all he uttered: the main business, indeed, of his
coming forth was frequently neglected and not seldom wholly
lost; but his excursions were so fanciful, so entertaining
and so ingenious, that no miscellaneous hearer, like myself,
could blame them.'

995. HMC, Dartmouth MSS, Eleventh Report, Appendix V (1887).
Mary, Lady Kenyon, to Lady Hanmer, 16th. February 1788 -
'... Mr. Burke, who is a wonderful speaker, though, I fear, a
very malignant man. I declare the impression his speech made
on me was that I would as soon choose to be the criminal, Mr.
Hastings, as the accuser. He seemed to dwell with such
pleasure on everything that was harsh and cruel.'

99. The Times, 20th. February 1788.
'The conclusion of Mr. Burke's oration was animated,
pathetic and replete with that energy and force of language
almost peculiar to himself.'

997. CEB, vol. V, pp. 426-432, 434-436, 445-447.
998. PB, pp. 225-226.
999. PM, pp. 176-181.
1000. JP, pp. 279-285.
1001. RM, pp. 317-318.
1002. SA, pp. 182-192.
1003. John W. Derry, The Regency Crisis and the Whigs (CUP,
    1936), passim.
1004. Christopher Hobhouse, Fox, pp. 188-193.
1005. S. Ayling. Fox: The Life of Charles James Fox, pp. 167-
    173, 187.
1006. S. Ayling, George III (Collins, 1972), pp. 344-345.
    Burke and the Regency Crisis, 1788-1789.

CEB, vol. V, p. 437.
    Burke to William Windham, c. 24th. January 1789, explaining
his absence from the House of Commons for a while and
retirement to Beaconsfield - 'I began to find that I was
grown rather too anxious; and had begun to discover to myself
and grown to others a solicitude relevant to the present
state of affairs, which though their strange condition might
well warrant it in others, is certainly less suitable to my
time of life, in which all emotions are less allowed ... I
sincerely wish to withdraw myself from this scene for good
and all.'

1008. Royal Archives (Windsor Castle), 38504-38505.
1009. A. Aspinall (ed.), The Correspondence of George, Prince
    of Wales, 1770-1812 (Cassell, 8 vols., 1963-1971),
    vol. II, p. 34.
1010. CEB, vol. VI, pp. 23-24.
1011. C.Hibbert, George IV (Penguin Books, 1967, pp. 142-143.
    Burke to Captain John Willett Payne (Prince George's
Private Secretary), 24th. September 1789, on the Prince's
visit to Yorkshire - '[It was the] happiest thing imaginable
and the best adapted to dispel prejudices in that county
which was cruelly poisoned with them. I hope that R,H. has
been pleased; indeed, I ought not to doubt it because I know
the benevolence of his character, and that he could not be
indifferent to the happiness he gave to so many people.'

1012. J. Wardroper, Kings, Lords and Wicked Libellers, Satire
    and Protest, 1760-1837) (John Murray, 1973), pp. 133-
    134.
    A handbill, stuck up in Whitehall after a violent speech

by Burke on the Regency question, which directly parodied the doctors' bulletins on the King - 'The Right Hon. Edmund Burke had last night three hours' sleep; he is calm this morning, but tending towards unquietness.'

1013. HMC, Thirteenth Report, Appendix VIII (Charlemont MSS), p. 106.
1014. CEB, vol. VI, pp. 9-12.
   Burke to the Earl of Charlemont, 9th. August 1789 - his earliest comment upon the storming of the Bastille in Paris on 14th. July 1789.

1015. CEB, vol. VI, pp. 27-28.
1016. A. Aspinall (ed.), The Correspondence of Prince George, vol. II, p. 37.
   Burke to Captain John Willett Payne, 1st. October 1789 - 'John Bull has been long dead and is succeeded by something not very much meriting that firm, blunt, thick-headed, but well-meaning title.'

1017. PR, vol. XXVII, p. 80.
1018. PD, vol. IXX, p. 72.
1019. PH, vol. XXVIII, c. 366.
1020. JP, pp. 299-300.
1021. SA, p. 220.
   Burke's first disagreement with Fox in Parliament, 9th. February 1790 - 'He could, without the least flattery or exaggeration, assure his right honourable friend, that the separation of a limb from his body could scarcely give him more pain than the circumstance of differing from him, violently and publicly, in opinion.'

1022. Bertram Newman, Edmund Burke, p. 207.
1023. London Chronicle, 16th. February 1790.
   'In the press and will speedily be published, Reflections on certain proceedings of the Revolution Society of the 4th. November 1789, concerning the affairs of France.'

1024. J. Parkes & H. Merivale (eds.), Memoirs of Sir Philip Francis, vol. II, p. 264.
   Francis to Burke, 13th. December 1789 on the trial of Hastings - 'What is the conduct of our pretended friends? Put an end to the Trial! You have spun it out too long! The people are tired of it! ... I have done with that sort of friends.'

1025. Robin Myers (ed.), The Autobiography of Luke Hansard, Printer to the House, 1752- 1828 (Printing Historical Society, 1991), p. 29.
   Luke Hansard's assistance in printing the early editions of the Philosophical Enquiry and Reflections on the Revolution in France.

1026. John Brooke, King George III (Constable, 1972), p. 345.
   King George III on Burke's Reflections - 'Read it; it will do you good; it is a book which every gentleman ought to read.'

1027. JP, p. 315.
   William Wilberforce - 'Burke's book is a most admirable medicine against the French disease.'

1028. Fitzwilliam correspondence, vol. III, pp. 171ff.
1029. Countess of Minto, Life of Sir Gilbert Eliot, vol. I, p. 365.
1030. Memoirs of Richard Cumberland, vol. II, p. 272.
1031. Austin Dobson (ed.), Diary and Letters of Mme. D'Arblay 6 vols., 1905), vol. IV, p. 435.
1032. BL, Add. MSS. 37483, f. 19. [William Windham].
1033. R. Blunt, Mrs. Montagu 'Queen of the Blues', (2 vols., 1932), vol. II, p. 248.
   Further appreciations of Burke's Reflections.

1034. Edward Lascelles, The Life of Charles James Fox, (OUP, 1936, p. 182.
   A copy of Burke's Reflections sent to Fox, with the author's compliments, but no record of his reaction.

1035. The Times, 2nd. November 1790.
   'Whatever may have been the political errors of its author, this work may be truly said to redeem them all.'

1036. Thomas Paine, Rights of Man (1791), p. 26.
   '[Burke] is not affected by the validity of distress touching his heart, but by the show resemblance of it striking his imagination. He pities the plumage, but forgets the dying bird.'

1037. Edward Gibbon, Autobiography (Everyman, 1939), p. 178.
1038. Bertram Newman, Edmund Burke, p. 228.
1039. J.C. Morison, Gibbon (Macmillan. 1909), p. 139.
   Edward Gibbon - 'I beg leave to subscribe my assent to Mr. Burke's creed on the revolution in France. I admire his eloquence, I approve his politics, I adore his chivalry, and I can almost excuse his reverence for church establishments.'

1040. Samuel Parr, A Sequel to the Printed Paper Lately Circulated in Warwickshire by the Rev. Charles Curtis, A Birmingham Rector, etc. (1791), p. 63.
1041. Warren Derry, Dr. Parr, p. 138.
   Dr. Samuel Parr - 'Upon the first perusal of Mr. Burke's book, I felt, like many other men, its magical force; and, like many other men, I was at last delivered from the illusions which had cheated my reason and borne from admiration to assent.'

1042. CEB, vol. VI, pp. 85-87.
1043. J. Parkes & H. Merivale (eds.), Sir Philip Francis (3 vols., 1867), vol. III, p. 130.
1044. PM, p. 200.
1045. RM, p. 351.
   Sir Philip Francis to Burke, 17th. January 1790 - 'In my opinion, all you say of the Queen is pure foppery. If she be a pure female character, you ought to take your ground upon her virtues. If she be the reverse, it is ridiculous, in any but a lover, to place her personal charms in opposition to

her crimes .... Pray, Sir, how long have you felt yourself so
desperately disposed to admire the ladies of Germany?'

1046. CEB, vol. VI, pp. 88-92.
1047. A. Cobban, Edmund Burke, p. 121.
1048. SA, p. 201.
     Burke to Francis, 20th. February [1790] - 'What! - are not
high rank, great splendour of descent, great personal
elegance and outward accomplishments, ingredients of moment
in forming the interests we take in the misfortunes of men?
... I tell you again, - that the recollection of the manner
in which I saw the Queen of France, in the year 1774
[actually in 1773] and the contrast between that brilliancy,
splendour and beauty, with the prostrate of a nation to her,
compared with the abominable scene of 1789 which I was
describing, did draw tears from me and wetted my paper. These
tears came again into my eyes almost as often as I looked at
the description.'

1049. A.R. Waller & Arnold Glover, The Collected Works of
     William Hazlitt (Dent, 12 vols., 1902-1906), 'Arguing
     in a Circle (1823),' vol. XI, p. 290.
'The author of the Reflections has seen or dreamt he saw a
most delightful vision sixteen years before, which has thrown
his brain into a ferment; and he was determined to throw his
readers and the world into one too. It was a theme for a copy
of verses or a romance; not for a work in which the destinies
of mankind were to be weighed. Yet she was the Helen that
opened another Iliad of wars; and the world has paid for that
accursed glance at youthful beauty with rivers of blood.'

1050. Mrs. Paget Toynbee (ed.), Letters of Horace Walpole (16
     vols., 1903-1905), vol. XIV, p. 329.
1051. Bertram Newman, Edmund Burke, p. 212.
     Horace Walpole - 'I know the tirade on the Queen of France
is condemned, and yet I must own I admire it much. It paints
her exactly as she appeared to me the first time I saw her
when Dauphiness. She...shot through the room like an aerial
being.'

1052. A. Aspinall (ed.), op. cit., vol. II, p.136n.
     On 30th. November 1790, Henry Temple, second Viscount
Palmerston, dined with Burke, who was 'in very good spirits
and talked a good deal about his book, which made [William]
Windham look grave and shake his head, though he avoided any
altercation.'

1053. George Rous, Thoughts on Government (1790).
1054. Catherine Macaulay, Observations on the Reflections of
     the Right Honourable Edmund Burke on the Revolution of
     France (1790).
1055. Capel Lofft, Remarks on the Letter of the Right
     Honourable Edmund Burke (1790).
1056. James Mackintosh, Vindiciae Gallicae (1791).
1057. Thomas Paine, The Rights of Man, 2 parts (1791 & 1792).
     [A convenient reprint of both parts, ed. Henry Collins
(Penguin Books, 1969].

1058. Joseph Priestley, Letters to the Right Honourable Edmund Burke, occasioned by his 'Reflections on the Revolution in France'. (1791).
1059. Sir Brooke Boothby, A Letter to the Right Honourable Edmund Burke (1791).
1060. Thomas Christie, Letters on the Revolution in France (1791).
1061. Answer to the Reflections of Mr. Edmund Burke. By M. Depont (1791). [Yale University Library has a copy].
1062. William Wordsworth, Letter to the Bishop of Llandaff (1793).
    Answers to Burke's Reflections.

1063. S, First Series, vol. III, p. 83: 6th. May 1791.
    Burke - 'Societies were formed to recommend Paine's Rights of Man and Mackintosh's Vindication of the French Revolution, and other abominable and dangerous publications, to the attention of the people, factioned by a falsehood and forgery, the pretended authority of Government.'

1064. P.P.Howe (ed.), Complete Works of William Hazlitt, (Centenary Edition, Dent, 21 vols., 1930-1934), vol. VII, pp. 306-307.
1065. John W. Kinnaird, William Hazlitt, Critic of Power, Columbia University Press, New York, 1978), pp. 106-110. 126.
    Hazlitt's consideration of Burke's Reflections.

1066. P. O'Leary, Sir James Mackintosh, p. 22.
    Thomas Campbell - 'In the better educated classes of society, there was a general proneness to go with Burke, and it is my sincere opinion, that the proneness would have become universal, if such a mind of Mackintosh's had not presented itself like a breakwater to the general springtide of Burkeism ... without disparagement to Paine, in a great and essential view, it must be admitted that, though radically sound in sense, he was deficient in the strategies of philosophy; whilst Mackintosh met Burke perfectly his equal in the tactics of moral science and in beauty of style and illustration. Hence Mackintosh went, as the apostle of liberalism, among a class - perhaps too influential in society - to whom the manner of Paine was repulsive.'

1067. Canning Papers, William L. Clements Library, Ann Arbor, Michigan.   George Canning to Lord Crewe, 25th. May 1791.
1068. Peter Dixon, Canning, Politician and Statesman (Weidenfeld & Nicolson, 1976), p. 13.
    Canning's early approval of Sir James Mackintosh's answer to Burke's Reflections.

1069. Ralph. M. Wardle, William Hazlitt (University of Nabraska Press, Lincoln, 1971), pp. 51-52.
    Hazlitt's comparison between Mackintosh and Burke - 'Mackintosh was no match for Burke, either in style or matter. Burke was an orator (almost a poet), who reasoned in

figures, because he had an eye for nature: Mackintosh, on the other hand, was a rhetorician, who had only an eye to common-places.

1070. <u>The Times</u>, 5th. November 1790.
Report of Horne Tooke's speech at the Revolution Society - 'Out of regard for Mr. Burke (says he) let us wish that if it be his lot to be tried - (for having published the truth we suppose) his trial may last as long as that of Mr. Hastings.'

1071. Edward Tatham, <u>Letters to the Rt. Hon. Edmund Burke on Politics</u> (1791).
1072. V.H.H. Green, <u>Oxford Common Room</u> (Edward Arnold, 1957).
A series of published letters by Edward Tatham, Rector of Lincoln College, Oxford, seeking to supplement Burke's arguments in the <u>Reflections</u> - 'Availing themselves of the confusion which prevails in a neighbouring kingdom, they come out as an antidote to that slow poison which has been so industriously administered and insinuated with such consummate art in the veins of our countrymen by a set of phlegmatic politicians.'

1073. CEB, vol. VI, pp. 203-204.
1074. SA, p. 202.
Edward Jerningham to Burke, 18th. January 1791, describing Marie Antoinette's reading of his account of her in a French translation of the <u>Reflections</u> - 'One of the Queen's bedchamber women carried it to the Queen, who before she had read half the lines, she burst into a flood of tears, and was a long time before she was sufficiently composed to peruse the remainder.'

1075. George Rude, <u>Revolutionary Europe 1783-1815</u> (Fontana History of Europe, 1964), pp. 195, 300.
The influence of the <u>Reflections</u> in Europe.

1076. Lord John Russell (ed.), <u>Memorials and Correspondence of Charles James Fox</u> (4 vols., 1853-1857), vol. II, p. 363.
1077. Stanley Ayling, <u>Fox</u> (John Murray, 1991), p. 172.
Charles James Fox on Burke's <u>Letter to a Member of the National Assembly</u> (1791) - 'I have not read Burke's new pamphlet.... It is in general to be thought mere madness, and especially in those parts where he is for a general war for the purpose of destroying the general government of France.'

1078. PH, vol. IXXX, c. 387.
1079. CEB, vol. VI, pp. 255, 273, 291; vol. IX, pp. 445-446.
1080. RM, pp. 375-376.
1081. JP, pp. 329-336.
1082. Lord John Russell, <u>Memorials and Correspondence of Charles James Fox</u> (2 vols., 1852), vol. II, pp. 11-12.
1083. PM, pp. 213-220.
1084. SA, pp. 218-220.

1085. Edward Lascelles, The Life of Charles James Fox (OUP, 1936), pp. 225-228.
1086. Christopher Hobhouse, Fox (John Murray, 1964), pp. 194-197.
1087. David Powell, Charles James Fox (Hutchinson. 1989), pp. 197-199.
1088. Stanley Ayling, Fox, pp. 170-173.
1089. R. Therry, A Letter to George Canning, to which are annexed Six Letters of Edmund Burke (1826), p. 60.
     The final rift between Burke and Fox, 6th. May 1791 - 'He knew the price of his conduct; he had done his duty at the price of his friend; their friendship was at an end.'

1090. Morning Chronicle, 12th. May 1791.
1091. JP, p. 347n.
1092. PM, p. 220.
     'The great and firm body of the Whigs of England, true to their principles, have decided upon the dispute between Mr. Fox and Mr. Burke; and the former is declared to have maintained the pure doctrine by which they are bound together, and upon which they have invariably acted. The consequence is that Mr. Burke retires from Parliament.'

1093. J. E. Norton (ed.), The Letters of Edward Gibbon (Cassell, 3 vols., 1956), vol. III, p. 229.
     Gibbon to Lord Sheffield, 25th. May 1791 - 'Poor Burke is the most rational and eloquent madman I ever knew. I love Fox's feelings, but I detest the political principles of the man and of the party.'

1094. Edmund Burke, Letter to the Chevalier de Rivarol, 1st. June 1791.
1095. E.J. Hobsbawm, The Age of Revolution 17898-1848 (Mentor Books, New York), p. 291.
     'It were better to forget, once for all, the encyclopedie and the whole body of economists and to revert to those old rules and principles which have hitherto made princes great and nations happy.'

1096. HMC, Dartmouth MSS, Eleventh Report, Appendix V (1887), p. 535.
     Lord Erskine to Lord Kenyon, August 1791 - 'I have left you Burke's pamphlet [Appeal from the New to the Old Whigs], which, though perfidious to his friends by imputing sentiments to them which they never held, in order to disgrace them, has yet in it some very splendid passages.'

1097. S, First Series, vol. V, p. 809 - 11th. May 1792.
     'With respect to the Bastille, the destruction of which Mr. Burke had so feelingly lamented, Mr. Fox expressed his exultation at the destruction of that diabolical prison .... [Here Mr. Burke rose in a great hurry and passed from the Opposition side of the House and placed himself by Mr. Pitt, accompanied by a very hearty laugh from the House].'

1098. Joyce Henlow (ed.), The Journals and Letters of Fanny Burney (10 vols., 1972), vol. I, p. 178.
     30th. May 1792 - 'When the impetuous and ungovernable Mr.

Burke was interrupting the Chancellor in order to brow-beat
Mr. Hasting's evidence, Mr. Windham, involuntarily exclaimed,
"Hist!' just as if he had been at his elbow and playing the
kind part of a flapper.'

1099. Thomas Paine, <u>A Letter Addressed to his Addressors</u>
(1792).
'As he [Burke] rose like a rocket, he fell like a stick.'

1100. BL, Add. MSS. 9828. Burke to John Eardley Wilmot,
2nd. October 1792.
1101. Margery Weiner, <u>The French Exiles 1789-1815</u>.
Burke's support for the Fund for the Relief of the
Suffering Clergy of France in the British Dominions.

1102. PR, vol. XXXIV, p. 224.
1103. PH, vol. XXX, c. 189,
1104. S, First Series, , vol. V, p. 156.
1105. <u>Morning Post</u>, 29th. December 1792
1106. <u>Sheffield Register</u>, 18th. January 1793.
1107. CEB, vol. VII, pp. 328, 340.
1108. Horace Twiss, <u>Life of Lord Eldon</u> (1846), vol.I,p. 152.
1109. R. Chambers (ed.), <u>The Book of Days</u> (2. vols, 1865),
vol. I, p. 36.
1110. JP, pp.367-368.
1111. SA, p. 248.
Burke's dagger scene in Parliament, 28th. December 1792 -
'Mr. Burke drew a dagger from his breast, which, after he had
wielded in a theatrical manner, he flung against the floor,
pointing down at it, saying, "This is what you are to gain by
an alliance with France;" he then took it up and kept it
elevated in his right hand during the remainder of his
speech.'

1112. Nina, Countess of Minto (ed.), <u>Life and Letters of Sir
Gilbert Elliot, First Earl of Minto from 1751 to 1806</u>
3 vols, 1874), vol. II, pp. 170-173.
Burke to Elliot, September 1793, urging the sending of
assistance to the Royalists in Brittany - 'These brave and
principled men, with very inadequate means, have struggled,
and hitherto victoriously, for upwards of six months and have
...done more against the common enemy...than all the regular
armies of Europe.... They amount to about 40,000, though ill-
armed and ill-provided.... Where can we hope to plant about
40,000 men in the heart of the enemy's country at less than a
hundred times what the support of that would come to?'

1113. <u>An Address to the Hon. Edmund Burke from the
Swinish Multitude</u> (1793), quoted E.P. Thompson, <u>The
Making of the English Working Class</u> (Penguin
Books, 1968), p.98.
'Whilst ye are...gorging yourselves at troughs filled with
the daintiest wash; we, with our numerous train of
porkers, are employed, from the rising to the setting sun to
obtain the means of subsistence, by...picking up a few
acorns.'

LAST YEARS (1794-1797)

1114. CEB, vol. VII, pp. 553, 554-555.
1115. JP, p. 391.
Burke's retirement from Parliament.

1116. Philip Henry, Earl Stanhope, Life of the Right
Honourable William Pitt (4 vols., 1862), vol. II, p.
244.
1117. Burke and Windham Correspondence, p. 109.
The proposed peerage for Burke, 1794.

1118. CEB, vol. VI, pp. 563-566.
1119. JP, p. 395.
1120. RM, pp. 392-394.
1121. SA, pp. 255-256.
Death of Burke's son, Richard, 2nd. August 1794.

1122. Bonamy Dobree (ed.), The Letters of King George III
(Cassell, 1935), p. 225.
1123. A. Aspinall (ed.), Later Correspondence of George III
(5 vols., 1963), vol. II, pp. 238, 244-245.
1124. J.H. Rose, Pitt and Napoleon (1912), p. 238.
1125. AS, p. 257.
1126. Robert John Auckland, third Baron, Bishop of Bath and
Wells (ed.), The Journal and Correspondence of William,
Lord Auckland (4 vols., 1862), vol. III, pp. 319-320.
George III to Pitt, 5th. September 1794, on receiving
Burke's acknowledgement of the award of his pension –
'Misfortunes are the greatest softeners of the human mind:
and have in the instance of this distressed man made him own
what his warmth of temper would not have allowed under other
circumstances, viz, that he may have erred. One quality I
take him to be very susceptible of, that is gratitude, which
covers many failings, and makes me therefore very happy at
being able to relieve him.'

1127. Bonamy Dobree. op. cit., p. 235.
George III to Pitt, 6th. February 1795, about the scheme
for Roman Catholic emancipation put forward by Lord
Fitzwilliam, Viceroy of Ireland – 'One might suppose the
authors of this scheme had not viewed the tendency or extent
of the question, but were actuated alone by the peevish
inclination of humiliating the old friends of English
government in Ireland, or from the desire of imputing implicit
obedience to the heated imagination of Mr. Burke.'

1128. Robin Reilly, Pitt the Younger Cassell, 1978), p. 242.
Burke to Auckland on his pamphlet (1795) advocating peace
with France – '[It] has filled me with a degree of grief and
dismay which I cannot find words to express... nothing can be
the consequence but utter and irretrievable ruin.'
Pitt to Auckland – 'I return Burke's letter, which is like
other rhapsodies from the same pen, in which there is much to
admire and nothing to agree with.'

1129. BL, Add. MSS. 37843, f. 105.
1130. JP, pp. 433-436.
1131. RM, pp. 389-390.

1132. SA, pp. 259, 274-275.
1133. Sir   John   Mackintosh, Memoirs (2 vols., 1835),   vol.
     I, pp. 87-94.
1134. Margaret Weiner, The French Exiles, pp. 126-127.
1135. J.Gilbert Jenkins, A History of the Parish of Penn
     (1935).
     Burke's emigre school at Penn.

1136. CEB, vol. VIII, p. 446n1.
1137. JP, p. 435.
     Burke's disciplinary   advice   to   the   master   at the
Penn school - 'You must exert your cane with more vigour,
and if that does not do, you must flog - and flog soundly. Do
not fear its success. It is our chief receipt in England for
turning out eminent men - it seldom fails - good scholars,
nay good poets, are made by the rod - and why not good
soldiers?'

1138. J. Parkes & H. Merivale (eds.), Memoirs of Sir Philip
     Francis (2 vols, 1867), vil. II, p.246.
     Burke to Francis during the last months of his life - 'If
a man is disabled from rendering any essential service to his
principles or to his party, he ought at least contrive to
make his conversation as little disagreeable as he can to the
society which his friends may still be indulgent enough to
hold with him.'

1139. P.P. Howe, The Life of William Hazlitt   (Penguin Books,
     1949), p. 52.
     Hazlitt's comment on reading Burke's Letter to a Noble
Lord (1796) - 'I said to myself, "This is true eloquence;
this is a man pouring out his mind on paper".'

1140. CEB, vol. IX, p. 114.
1141. SA, p. 280.
     Burke to John Keogh, 17th. November 1796 - 'Contrary to
all reason, experience and observation, many persons in
Ireland have taken it into their heads that the influence of
the Government here has been the cause of the misdemeanours
of persons in power in that country and that they are
suffering under the yoke of a British dominion - I must speak
the truth - I must say that all the evils of Ireland
originate within itself ... England has hardly anything to do
with Irish government. I heartily wish it were otherwise.'

1142. CEB, vol. IX, pp. 194-196.
1143. James Mackintosh, Memoirs, vol. I, pp. 87, 91-92.
1144. P. O'Leary, Sir James Mackintosh, p. 37.
1145. Bertram Newman, Edmund Burke, p. 329.
     James Mackintosh's visit to the house-bound Burke at
Beaconsfield, Christmas 1796 - Burke entered 'with cordial
glee into the sports of the children, rolling about with them
on the carpet and pouring out, in his gambols, the sublimist
images, mingled with the most wretched puns'.

1146. Bertram Newman, Edmund Burke, p. 335.
     Wilberforce on his visit to Burke, 17th. April 1797-
'Heard of the Portsmouth mutiny [of the fleet] consultation
with Burke .... The whole scene is now before me. Burke was

lying on a sofa much emaciated, and Windham, Laurence and
some other friends were around him. The attention shown to
Burke by all that party was just like the treatment of
Ahitoophel of old; it was as if one went to inquire of the
oracle of the Lord.'

1147. Countess of Minto (ed.), Sir Gilbert Elliot, vol. II,
      p. 415.
      Elliot on Burke's dying days - 'He is emaciated to the
greatest degree, has lost entirely his powers of digestion.
He considers his own case quite desperate and is rather
irritated than flattered by the supposition of his recovery
being possible.'

1148. CEB, vol. IX, pp. 372-373.
1149. JP, p. 456.
1150. SA, p. 281.
1151. David Powell, Charles James Fox, p. 242
      Burke's rejection of Fox's attempt to arrange a last
reconciliatory meeting with him.

1152. Robert Isaac and Samuel Wilberforce, The Life of
      William Wilberforce (5 vols., John Murray, 1838),
      vol. II, p. 208.
      Henry Thornton to Hannah More - 'Burke spent much of the
last two days of his life reading Wilberforce's book
[A Practical View of the Prevailing Religious System of
Professed Christians in the Higher and Middle Classes of
this Country contrasted with Real Christianity (1797)] and
said that he derived much comfort from it.'

1153. Sir Arthur Bryant, The Years of Endurance 1793-
      1802 (Fontana, 1961).
      Burke's dying words on the wartime situation - 'Never
succumb to these difficulties. It is a struggle for your
existence as a nation, and, if you die, die with the world in
your hand.'

1154. Gentleman' Magazine, vol. LXIX (pt. i), p. 621.
      The death of Burke - 'His end was suited to the simple
greatness of mind which he displayed through life, every way
unaffected, without levity, without ostentation, full of
natural grace and dignity.'

1155. The Times, 11th. July 1797.
1156. London Chronicle, 8th.-11th, July 1797.
1157. Morning Chronicle, 10th. July 1797.
1158. Lloyd's Evening Post, 10th.-12th. July 1797,
      Eulogy of Burke by Walker King, who 'long and intimately
knew him.'

1159. CEB, vol. I, p. 357.
      Burke to Michael Smith, c. 1750 -   'I would rather sleep
in the southern corner of a little country churchyard than in
the tomb of the Capulets. I should like, however, that my
dust should mingle with kindred dust.'

1160. PM, p. 297.
  Burke's will, desiring to be buried 'in the Church at
Beaconsfield near to the bodies of my dearest brother and my
dearest son, in all humility praying that, as we have lived
in perfect unity, we may together have a part   in   the
resurrection of the just.'

1161. BL, Add. Mss. 32566 - unpublished papers of L. J.
    Mitford.
1162. 'The Grave of Edmund Burke,' Notes and Queries, vol.
    CXLIX, p. 80.
1163. T.W, Copeland, Edmund Burke, Six Essays, pp. 90-91.
1164. SA, p. 281.
  'Burke buried in a wooden coffin. Afraid the French should
find his body; his bones moved from that coffin to a leaden
one later.'

1165. Sir   Charles   Petrie,   George   Canning   (Eyre and
    Spottiswoode, 2nd. ed., 1946), p. 44.
  Canning writing in a letter, 13th. July 1797 - 'There is
only one piece of news, but that is news for the world.
Burke is dead.'

1166. Sir Robert Dallas, defence counsel for Warren Hastings,
    in Farington Diary, vol. II, p. 102n.
      'Oft have I wondered why on Irish ground
      No poisonous reptile yet was found;
      Reveal'd the secret of Nature's work -
      She saved her venom to create a Burke.'

1167. Samuel   Taylor   Coleridge,   Monody   on   the   Death   of
    Chatterton (1797).
      'Yet never, Burke, thou drankst Corruption bowl!
      Thee stormy Pity and the cherished lure
      Of Pomp and proud Precipitance of soul
      Wildered with meteor fires. Ah, Spirit pure!
      The error's mist had left they purged eye:
      So might I clasp thee with a Mother's joy.'

1168. Oliver Goldsmith, Retaliation (1774).
      'Here lies our good Edmund, whose genius was such
      We scarcely can praise it or blame it too much;
      Who, born for the Universe, narrowed his mind,
      And to party gave up what was meant for mankind.'

1169. C. Hobhouse, Fox, pp. 260-261.
1170. P. O'Leary, Sir James Mackintosh, p. 65.
  Fox's refusal in 1802 to support a plan for a memorial to
Burke because he could not pretend to forgive his Conduct on
the Minority.

1171. A Catalogue of the Library of ... Edmund Burke;
    The Library the late Sir M.B. Clare, M.D.; Some Articles
    from Gibbon's Library .... Sold by Auction by Mr.
    Evans .... Thursday, November 7 ... 1833.
  The copy of this catalogue in the British Library lists
the purchasers of the different items.

LATER JUDGEMENTS UPON BURKE

1172. R.J. McHugh, <u>Henry Grattan</u> (Duckworth, 1936), p. 104.
Henry Grattan - 'He [Burke] was so fond of arbitrary power
that he could not sleep on his pillow unless he thought the
king had a right to take it from under him.'

1173. David Powell, <u>Charles James Fox</u>, pp. 74-75.
Charles James Fox applying Burke's <u>Conciliation with the
Colonies</u> (1774), when urging parliamentary reform in 1792 -
'Let gentlemen read this speech by day and meditate on it
by night; let them peruse it again and again, study it,
imprint it on their minds, impress it on their hearts - they
would there learn that representation was the sovereign
remedy for every evil.'

1174. Sir Charles Petrie, <u>Lord Liverpool and his Times</u>
(James Barrie, 1954), p. 150.
Lord Liverpool opposing parliamentary reform in 1810 -
'He would say that he believed there never was a period
in our history when the representation of the people in
Parliament was less unequal. That it was unequal in
theory he would admit, but that theoretic inequality
he regarded as one of the greatest advantages of
our constitution. This was the opinion of that
enlightened statesman, Mr. Burke, who said that it
was this peculiarity in its constitution which made it,
instead of an assembly of deputies, an entire and
perfect deliberative meeting.'

1175. William Wordsworth, <u>The Prelude</u> (completed 1805, but
published posthumously in 1850), Book VII, 1, 519
His mature attitude towards Burke:
'I see him, - old, but vigorous in age,-
Stand like an oak whose stag-horn branches start
Out of its leafy brow, the more to awe
The younger bretheren of the grove...
While he forewarns, denounces, launches forth
Against all systems built on abstract rights
Keen ridicule; the majesty proclaims
Of Institutes and Laws, hallowed by time;
Declares the vital power of social ties
Endeared by Custom; and with high disdain,
Exploding upstart Theory, insists
Upon the allegiance to which men are born.'

1176. August Wilhelm von Schlegel, <u>Lectures on Dramatic Art
and Literature</u> (trans. J. Black, 1815), vol. II, p. 278.
'He corrected his age when it was at the height of its
revolutionary frenzy; and without maintaining any system of
philosophy he seems to have seen farther into the true nature
of society and to have more clearly comprehended the effect
of religion in connecting individual security with national
welfare than any other philosopher or any system of
philosophy of any preceding age.'

1177. A.R. Waller & A. Glover, <u>op. cit.</u>, William Hazlitt,
'On Good Nature (9th. June 1816), vol. I. p. 105.

'The late Mr. Burke was an instance of an Irish patriot
and philosopher. He abused metaphysics because he could make
nothing out of them and turned his back upon liberty when he
found he could get nothing more by her.'

1178. Lord Brougham, <u>Historical Sketches of Statesmen</u> (1839),
     vol. I, pp. 303-304.
  'Is any man so blind as seriously to believe that, had Mr.
Burke and Mr. Fox been ministers of George III, they would
have resigned rather than try to put down the Americans?'

1179. D.C. Lathbury (ed.), <u>Correspondence on Church and
     Religion of William Ewart Gladstone</u> (John   Murray, 2
     vols., 1910, vol. II, p. 326.
  Gladstone   to   G.W.E.   Russell,   13th.   October   1884 -
'He [Burke] was perhaps the maker of the Revolutionary War;
and our going into that war perhaps made the Reign of Terror,
and, without any "perhaps" almost unmade the liberties, the
constitution and prosperity of our country. Yet I venerate
and almost worship him, though I can conceive it being argued
that all he did for freedom, justice, religion, purity of
government, in other respects and other quarters, were less
than the mischief which flowed out from the reflections.'

1180. Cambridge University Library, Acton MSS. 4967.
1181. RM, p. 407.
  Lord Acton - 'Burke loved to evade the arbitration of
principle. He was prolific of arguments that   were   admirable
but not decisive. He dreaded   two-edged   weapons   and   maxims
that   faced   both   ways.   Through   his   inconsistencies   we   can
perceive that his mind stood in a brighter light than his
language.... Half his genius was spent in making the secret
that hampered it. He was the most historically-minded of
English statesmen.'

1182. <u>Letters of Lord Acton to Mary Gladstone</u>, pp. 56-57.
1183. David Mathew, <u>Acton, The Formative Years</u> (Eyre &
     Spottiswoode, 1956), p. 6.
  Lord Acton - 'You can hardly imagine what Burke is for all
of us who think about politics and are not wrapped in the
blaze   and   whirlwind   of   Rousseau.   Systems   of   scientific
thought   have   been   built   up   by   famous   scholars   on   the
fragments that fell from his table. Great literary fortunes
have been made by men who traded on the hundredth part of
him.'

1184. F.J.C. Hearnshaw, <u>Political Ideas</u> (Nelson, new   ed.,
     1937), pp. 101-102.
  'He was a practical statesman rather than a political
theorist. He wrote on the urgent problems of the day when and
as they arose. But he had an amazing faculty for penetrating
beneath   the   surface   of   things   and   for   seeing,   below   the
temporary   expedients   and   the   shifty   arguments   of   the
politician, the eternal truths of the philosopher. He never
rested until he had discovered the fundamental principles by
means of which the particular proposals of his party could be
justified. Hence his writings are more rich in practical
guidance for men of affairs than those of any other political
thinker.

BURKE'S CHARACTER

Breadth of Knowledge

1185. William Stanhope Taylor and Captain John Henry
    Pringle (eds.). Correspondence of William Pitt, Earl of
    Chatham (3 vols., London, 1839), vol. III, p. 110.
    Duke of Grafton to Earl of Chatham, 16th. October 1766 -
Burke is 'the readiest man upon all points perhaps in the
whole House [of Commons].'

1186. James Boswell, The Life of Dr. Johnson, vol. I, p. 619.
    Dr. Johnson (1776) - 'Burke is an extraordinary man. His
stream of mind is perpetual.'

1187. James Boswell, The Journal of a Tour to the Hebrides
    with Samuel Johnson (OUP, 1930), p. 267.
    Dr. Johnson (1773) - 'Burke has great knowledge, great
fluency of words and great prompness of ideas, so that he can
speak with great illustration on any subject that comes
before him.'

1188. JP, p. 486.
    The Revd. Thomas Campbell - 'His learning is so various
and extensive that we might praise it for its range and
compass were it not still more praiseworthy for its solidity
and depth. His imagination is so lively and creative that he
may justly be called the child of fancy.'

Hotness of Temper

1189. CEB, vol. II, pp. 124-125, 127.
1190. SA, p. 51.
    Thomas Allan to Sir George Macartney, March 1770 - 'There
were high words in the House of Commons on Thursday between
Mr. Edmund Burke and Mr. Rigby, exceeding gross on both
sides, the former in better language, the latter very plain,
said he was a scoundrel.'

1191. Lord John Russell, Memorials and Correspondence of Fox
    vol. I, p. 146.
1192. Parliamentary History, vol. XVI, pp. 919-921, 923-924.
1193. JP, p. 172.
1194. SA, p. 51.
    Mr. Crawford to Lord Ossory, December 1777 - 'There were
high words between Wedderburn [the Attorney-General] and
Burke, which so offended the latter that he went out of the
House [of Commons], and I believe intended to challenge
Wedderburn [to a duel], but was prevented by a letter from
Wedderburn and an explanation likewise which he sent through
Charles [James Fox].'

1195. HMC, Fourteenth Report, Appendix 1 (1894), p. 110.
    Thomas Orde to the Duke [of Rutland], 17th. June 1784 -
'Burke, after five fruitless efforts to gain the permission
of the House [of Commons] to be heard, broke away in a
violent passion and did not return to vote at all.'

Compassion

1196. CEB, vol. VI, pp. 8-9.
    Burke to William Wyndham Grenville, 4th. August 1789, on
behalf of an Irishman sentenced to Botany Bay for theft -
'As a case in which there are circumstances of doubt or
alleviation, when you consider how much the punishment of
transportation is aggravated beyond what formerly it has
been, you will I dare say think with me that there may be
groundfor pardon with or without conditions, as you may thin
reasonable, and that you will be pleased to comply with the
wishes of so many respectable people as seem concerned for
this poorman on whose life and industry a large family
depends.'

Moodiness

1197. CEB, vol. II, p. 374.
    Burke to the Duke of Richmond, 15th. November 1772 -
'the occasional dejections and vexations I am subject to'.

Oratory

1198. Charles Petrie, When Britain Saved Europe (1943), p.88.
1199. Arthur Bryant, The Years of Endurance 1793-1802, p.74.
    John Wilkes - 'Just as the Venus of Appelles suggested
milk and honey, so Burke's oratory is reminiscent of whisky
and potatoes.'

1200. James Boswell, Life of Johnson, vol. I, p. 396.
    Dr. Johnson (1770) - 'It was commonly observed he [Burke]
spoke too often in parliament; but nobody could say he did
not speak well, though too frequently and too familiarly.'

1201. Paul H. Emden, Regency Pageant, p.122.
    George III during his illness - 'I am getting into Mr.
Burke's eloquence, saying too much on little things.'

1202. Sir Charles Petrie, The Four Georges, A Revaluation of
    Period from 1714 to 1830 (Eyre & Spottiswoode, 1935),
    p. 145
A Member of Parliament when Burke rose to speak with a
packet of papers in his hand - 'I do hope the honourable
gentleman does not mean to read that large bundle of papers
and bore us with a long speech into the bargain.'

1203. P.P Howe, The Life of William Hazlitt (Hamish Hamilton,
    1947), p. 26.
    William Hazlitt -'Burke's style was forked and playful as
the lightning, crested like the serpent. He delivered plain
things on a plain ground; but when he rose, there was no end
of his flights and curcumgyrations.'

1204. Henry Rogers, Works of Burke (1842) [Introduction].
    'Of many of the inferior accomplishments of an orator,
Burke was almost wholly destitute. His voice was harsh and
unmusical, his pronunciation strongly marked with his native
accent and his manner awkward.'

Writing

1205. Arthur Bryant, <u>Macaulay</u> (Peter Davies, 1932; Nelson 1938), p. 140.
     Lord Macaulay, after re-reading Burke, 'Admirable - the greatest man since Milton.'

Power of Conversation

1206. James Boswell, <u>Life of Johnson</u>, vol. I, p. 619.
     Dr. Johnson (1776) when ill - 'That fellow calls forth all my powers. Were I to see Burke now, it would kill me.'

1207. James Boswell, <u>op.cit.</u>, vol. II, p. 510.
     Dr.Johnson (1784) - 'If a man were to go by chance at the same time with Burke under a shed, to shun a shower, he would say - "this is an extraordinary man." If Burke should go into a stable to see his horse drest, the ostler would say - "we have an extraordinary man here."'

1208. James Boswell, <u>Journal of a Tour to the Hebrides,</u> pp. 179-180.
     Dr. Johnson (1773) - 'What I envy Burke for is, his being constantly the same. He is never what we call hum-drum; never unwilling to begin to talk, nor in haste to leave off....So desirous is he to talk, that, if one is speaking at the end of the table, he'll speak to somebody at the other end. Burke, sir, is such a man, that if you met him for the first time in a street where you were stopped by a drove of oxen, and you and he stepped aside to take shelter but for five minutes, h'd talk to you in such a manner, that, when you parted, you'd say, this is an extraordinary man.'

1209. Fanny Burney, <u>Diary</u> (1890).
     'Such Spirit - such Intelligence - so much energy when serious, so much pleasantry when sportive, - so manly conversation in his address, so animated in his conversation, so eloquent in Argument, so exhilarating in trifling - ! Oh, I shall rave about him till I tire you.'

1210. A.R. Waller & Arnold Glover, <u>op. cit.</u>, 'Character of Mr. Burke (5th. October 1815),' vol. III, p. 253.
     William Hazlitt - 'Burke's literary talents ... were his chief excellence. His style has all the familiarity of conversation and all the research of the most elaborate composition.'

Religious Beliefs

1211. Edmund Burke, <u>A Vindication of Natural Society</u> (1756), Preface.
     'The writers against religion, whilst they oppose every system, are wisely careful never to set up any of their own.'

1212. CEB, vol. II, pp. 298-299. Burke to the Countess of Huntingdon, 6th. February 1772.
     'I wish to see her [the Established Church's] walls raised on the foundation laid in the volume of divine truth, that

she may crush the conspiracy of Atheism and those principles which will not leave to religion even a toleration.

1213. Charles J. Abbey & John H. Overton, The English Church in the Eighteenth Century (Longmans, 1896).
    Burke in 1773 on John Leland, A View of the Principal Deistical Writers that have Appeared in England during the Last and Present Century (1754-1756) - 'The best book that has ever been written against these people is that in which the author has collected in a body the whole of the Infidel code and has brought their writings in one body to cut them all off together.'

1214. CEB, vol. IV, p. 261. Burke to Job Watts, 10th. August 1780.
    'I have been a steady friend since I came to the use of reason to the cause of religious toleration, not only as a Christian and a Protestant, but as once concerned for the civil defence of the country in which I live, and in which I have for some time discharged a publick trust.'

1215. Edmund Burke, Reflections on the Revolution in France (Everyman Edition), p. 10.
    'No sound ought to be heard in the church but the healing voice of Christian charity. The cause of civil liberty and civil government gains as little as that of religion by this confusion of duties. Surely the church is a place where one day's truce ought to be allowed to the dissensions and animosities of mankind.'

1216. Ibid, p. 27.
    'We know and it is our pride to know, that man is by his constitution a religious animal; that atheism is against, not only our reason, but our instincts; and that it cannot prevail long.'

1217. CEB, vol. VIII, p. 127. Burke to William Smith, 29th. January 1795.
    'Nothing is so fatal to religion as indifference, which is at least, half infidelity.'

Untidiness

1218. James Greig (ed.), The Farington Diary (2 vols., Hutchinson, 1922), vol. I, p. 192.
    'In his house Burke is quiet if not contradicted in any thing; but walks about heedless of every concern - knowing nothing of servants, expenses, etc. He is very careless of his papers - would drop on the floor a paper though it contained treason as he would do a newspaper cover. Mrs. Burke watches over everything, collects his scraps, arranges and dockets every paper.'

Author Index

Artist Index

The numbers cited are to item numbers, not to pages.

Subject Index

The numbers cited are to item numbers, not to pages.

Acton, Lord, 307, 1180-1183
American Revolution, 196, 219, 431, 433, 551-557, 627-
                    629, 838, 856-859, 877-880, 931-
                    933
Annual Register, 259, 282, 315, 589, 765-771, 1178

Barry, James, 191
Bastille, 1024, 1097
Bath
  Circus House, 590
  North Parade, 618
Beaconsfield, 272, 600, 826-833, 974-975
Blaise Castle, 606
Bristol, 184, 204, 274, 286, 287, 291-293, 605, 863-874,
        924-941
Burke, Edmund
  Appeal from the New to the Old Whigs (1791), 1096
  Assistant to Lord Rockingham (1765), 801, 802, 815, 816
  Assistant to W.G. Hamilton (1759-1764), 280, 788, 791-794
  Awarded Pension (1794), 236, 1122-1126
  Birth (1729), 581, 729-749
  Break with Fox, 1017-1021, 1034, 1077-1093, 1097, 1148-
                  1151, 1169, 1170.
  Characteristics, 1185-1218
  Death & Burial (1797), 1153, 1154, 1159-1164
  Declining Health, 1147
  Early Years, 179, 735-740
  Emigre School at Penn, 1132-1137
  Estimates of his Stature, 1172-1184
  Family, 716-720, 762-764
  Gordon Riots (1780), 910-915
  Letter to a Member of the National Assembly (1791), 1076,
                                                      1077
  Letter to a Noble Lord (1796), 1139
  Letter to the Chevalier de Rivarol (1791), 1094, 1095
  Marriage (1757), 775-778
  Middle Temple, London (1750-1755), 585, 757, 761
  M.P. for Bristol (1774-1780), 184, 204, 274, 286, 287, 291-
                                293, 605. 606, 863-874, 924-
                                941

About the Author

LEONARD W. COWIE was senior lecturer in history at both the University of London and the University of Surrey. He has written many books on British history.

ISBN 0-313-28710-4

90000>

ISBN 9 780313 287107

HARDCOVER BAR CODE